Nick Vandome

BUILDING A WEBSITE FOR SENIORS

in
easy steps

For the Over 50s

In easy steps is an imprint of Computer Step
Southfield Road · Southam
Warwickshire CV47 0FB · United Kingdom
www.ineasysteps.com

Notice of Liability
Every effort has been made to ensure that this book contains accurate
and current information. However, Computer Step and the author
shall not be liable for any loss or damage suffered by readers as a
result of any information contained herein.

Trademarks
All trademarks are acknowledged as belonging to their respective
companies.

Printed and bound in the United Kingdom

ISBN-13 978-1-84078-328-5
ISBN-10 1-84078-328-1

Contents

1 About websites

Websites are no longer just the domain of computer whizz-kids. This chapter gives an overview of types of websites and shows options for building and publishing them.

Why build a website

In the early days of the World Wide Web (WWW), the idea of publishing your own website was a daunting one. Both the price and the complexity of the technology was enough to put off all but the most dedicated computer professionals. This led to a certain mystic growing up about the construction of websites: it was in the interest of the people who made them, to keep the trade secrets close to their chests. As a result, certain consultants and companies made a lot of money from designing and building websites.

However, with the expansion of the Web, it soon became clear that the process of building websites was not as complex as some people suggested. In fact, instead of using complicated computer languages, websites are generally constructed with a language called Hypertext Markup Language (HTML). This is not a full-blown computer language, but rather a method of giving instructions to web browsers about how the page content is displayed. These instructions are contained within tags that are placed around the relevant content on the page. Initially, HTML pages for websites were created manually, i.e. people wrote the content for the pages and also the HTML code. Then programs were developed to help with the creation of HTML pages (HTML editors) and a further development was the appearance of What You See Is What You Get (WYSIWYG) web development programs. These are programs that allow users to create the pages without the need to know any HTML. The users lay out the pages as they want them to appear (in the same way as creating a page in a word processing program such as Word) and all of the HTML is created automatically in the background.

A further extension of WYSIWYG programs have been online services that allow people to build websites through web-based services. This is done through the use of pre-designed templates and it has so simplified the process of building websites that it is now possible for anyone to quickly and effectively construct their own website, regardless of their web authoring knowledge.

Don't forget

Websites can be built in a number of ways without having any knowledge of HTML. However, it is useful to know what it is and how it relates to the process of building websites.

Don't forget

Two of the most popular WYSIWYG programs are Frontpage from Microsoft and Dreamweaver from Adobe (formerly made by Macromedia).

Reasons for a website

Now that it is easier than ever to build your own website, it is worth looking at some of the reasons for doing this:

- Just out of curiosity. There is nothing wrong with building and publishing a website to learn some new skills and get a better understanding of the technology and terminology involved. However, it is still important to have some interesting content to include

- Displaying family information

- Publicizing your hobby

- Club or charity sites. If you are involved with a local club or charity, you will be a popular figure if you can offer to build a website. This could then be used to publish general information and up to date news about the organization

Updating websites

In some ways the easiest part of a successful website is building and publishing it in the first place. The real work starts once it is published and online for everyone to view on the World Wide Web. If a website is left unattended, users will become bored when they return to the site and discover that it is the same as before. It is therefore vital that websites, no matter what type they are, should be updated on a regular basis.

The first thing to remember about updating websites is that it takes a certain amount of time, but this does not need to be many hours every week. Look at your site and identify areas that can be updated on a weekly or monthly basis and then create a schedule that can be used for the updating functions. Sometimes updates will consist of a few new sentences or some additional photographs: at other times it may be a more fundamental overhaul. But it is important to take the time to update your site and also to tell people that it has been updated so that they know they are looking at fresh, new, material as often as possible.

Hot tip

When you are first planning your website, make sure that you have at least twice the amount of content that you think you will need. Then you can edit it down to the most relevant and interesting sections.

Website jargon explained

Although the language and terminology about the World Wide Web and websites has been modified and, in some instances, simplified since web design and creation was the domain of solely computer experts, there is still a lot of jargon associated with building and publishing websites:

- Accessibility. This is an area that is concerned with making websites available to people with disabilities, particularly blind and partially sighted users

- Blogs. This is a relatively recent phenomenon on the World Wide Web but one that has really caught on. Essentially a blog is an online diary which people update on a daily/weekly/monthly basis for anyone to look at

- Browsers. These are the programs that enable web pages to be viewed, in the same way as a television set enables television programs to be displayed. The most commonly used browser is Internet Explorer but other popular ones include Firefox and Apple's Safari

- Domain name. This is the unique name that is given to every website. A domain name applies to the whole site, not just individual pages

- Downloading. This is the process of copying something from a website onto your own computer. It can apply to photographs, music or video

- FTP. This stands for File Transfer Protocol and is the process for copying web pages from your own computer, onto an external computer of a service that is going to be hosting your website (see next item)

- Hosting service. This is an online company that stores your website and displays it so that everybody on the World Wide Web can view it, if they desire

- HTML. This stands for Hypertext Markup Language, which is used to create the instructions for browsers to interpret how they should display the content of web pages. The majority of web pages are created in HTML

Hot tip

Several browsers can be used on the same computer so that you can see which one you prefer for viewing web pages in terms of appearance and speed.

10

Don't forget

Most hosting services charge a fee for displaying your web pages on the World Wide Web.

- Hyperlinks. These are the links on web pages that enable you to move to another website, another page within the same site, or another part of the same page. By default they are frequently blue and underlined

- Internet. This is the collection of computers that are connected together around the world. It should not be confused with the World Wide Web: the Internet is the infrastructure on which the pages of the World Wide Web are displayed

- JPEG. This stands for Joint Photographic Experts Group and it is a common file format for displaying photographs on the web

- Navigation. This is the means for getting around a website. It is frequently in the form of a collection of buttons or links at the top or the side of a page

- Online publishing. This is the process of building and publishing a website from within a single online site, without the need to first create the files on your own computer

- Search engines. Programs for looking for websites, such as Google and Yahoo!

- Uploading. The process of copying files from your own computer onto those of a hosting service

- URL. This stands for Uniform Resource Locator and it is the unique name for every page on the Web

- Website. A collection of linked pages that, usually, share a common topic

- Wizards. Automated processes that can be used to build websites without the need for any HTML knowledge

- World Wide Web. The collection of websites and web pages that can be viewed from any computer that is connected to the Internet

Don't forget

On a lot of websites, hyperlinks are now more subtly produced than just being colored blue and underlined. For instance, many of them appear as normal text and a line appears under them when the cursor is passed over them. This is known as a rollover effect.

Don't forget

The most popular online publishing site is Yahoo! GeoCities. This is looked at in detail in Chapters 4, 5 and 6.

Options for website building

If you look at the World Wide Web you will see a wide variety of websites. Some are very professional and slick, while others are simpler and more down-to-earth. As the different types of sites suggests, there are different ways in which websites can be created.

Professional sites

These are usually created with dedicated web authoring software (or, in most cases, a combination of different programs) and can produce highly designed sites that contain elements, such as animation and dynamic features, that react to information that is entered by the user. These types of sites can be great to look at but it is not realistic to try and build them at home.

Beware

The more complicated and complex that a website is then the longer it will take to download and all of its components to appear completely.

HTML sites

HTML stands for Hypertext Markup Language. This is the coded language that is used to create most web pages. There are numerous programs that allow you to create your own HTML pages. Some of them, such as Dreamweaver or Frontpage, create the HTML for you as you build the content for pages, but programs such as this require some knowledge of HTML. Another drawback to this type of website building is that you will have to buy your own website address (domain name) and also find someone to host your website.

Online services

Online services are sites that provide you with the means to build your own website without the need to pay for web hosting or a domain name and you don't even have to know anything about HTML. The sites can be built using wizards that take you through the whole process with a series of templates into which your web content can be entered. Once the pages have been built, they are then automatically uploaded and published by the online service. The most popular online web publishing service is Yahoo! GeoCities.

Beware

Building pages in HTML can be a steep learning curve and it takes a considerable amount of time to become confident in building websites this way. However, it is also a very rewarding way to build websites, if you have the time.

13

Family websites

One of the most common, and the most satisfying, reasons for building your own website, is to publish information about your family. This can cover a number of areas:

- Family history. This can be a narrative history of the family and also a graphical family tree. This is one area that, once started, can provide years of research and investigation for anyone interested in becoming the family historian

- Family profiles. This can include information about family members, ideally provided by the individuals themselves

- Family news and photographs. This can include births and marriages and also photo galleries of family members and events

- Forthcoming events. This can include information about events such as family parties and holidays

As well as building your own family website, there are also online services that are aimed specifically at building family websites, such as MyFamily.com:

Club and hobby websites

For anyone with a hobby, or who is a member of a club or a charity, a website is an excellent idea. It is a great way to pass on information about your club or hobby, and to publish news and updates. The range of information that can be published on this type of website includes:

- Background and historical information. This can include general information about the club: when and why it was formed and the main events since its inception

- Contact details of club members. This can include details about how to join the club and the main club contacts

- Latest news. This can include news of recent events, competitions and all other news relating to the club

- Forthcoming events. This can include information about events, competition or outings

- Links to similar websites. This can include links to sites giving more information about the subject covered by the club and the website

Club websites should look welcoming and informative:

Website names

Every website on the World Wide Web has its own unique name so that it can be identified from every other page, in the same way that houses have their own addresses and zip codes. In the area of website names there are two main terms that are important: domain names and URLs.

Domain names

A domain name is a unique name that identifies a website, e.g. ineasysteps.com. This is what you register and pay for if you want to have a specific domain name for your website, such as nickvandome.com. There are numerous online sites that enable you to register domain names and they all have their own pricing structures. Domain names also include the extension, e.g. .com, .org, .net or .tv. Therefore, nickvandome. com and nickvandome.org are both different domain names and they can both be registered separately.

All websites have their own domain names, but you do not have to register your own domain name to publish a website. If you use an online service, such as Yahoo! GeoCities, the domain name will be that of the service, i.e. geocities.com. Once you have created your own site, your own name will be added to the domain name of the online service, i.e. geocities.com/nickvandome/index.htm

URLs

URL stands for Uniform Resource Locator and this is the unique identifier for each individual page on the World Wide Web. This includes the domain name of the site and also the address of specific pages. URLs also include http:// www. at the beginning of a web address. So, in the example above, the URL for the main GeoCities page could be http://www.geocities.com/ while the URL for subsequent pages would be http://www.geocities.com/nickvandome. index.htm etc. Each subsequent page within the site will also have its own unique URL. In all cases the domain name is still geocities.com

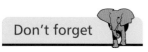

Don't forget

When you use an online service, your registration details will be used to create the URL for your website.

Publishing a website

If you use an online website service, the publishing of the site will be undertaken during the site building process with the online wizard. This means that once you have finished building your site, and you are happy with the content, the site can immediately be made available to anyone viewing the World Wide Web. With services such as GeoCities, sites can be published at the same time as when a file is saved:

However, if you have your own domain name and have built your own site in HTML, or with a web authoring program, you will have to find an online hosting service. These are companies to which you can send your web pages and they will store them on their computers and display them on the World Wide Web on your behalf.

If you are using a hosting service, you will have to physically copy your web page files from your computer onto the computers of the service that is hosting your website. This is usually done with a process called FTP (File Transfer Protocol) and consists of a command to copy over your files to the external hosting service. To do this, certain settings and passwords are required but these will be provided by the hosting service. A lot of web authoring programs have a built-in FTP function and once the settings have been entered, it is usually just a case of clicking one button. Although publishing a website with a hosting service is a bit more complicated than with an online website service, it is not as daunting as it may first seem and should always be kept in mind as an option.

Publicizing your website

Once your website has been published you will want to let people know about it so that they can look at it. This can be done in a number of ways:

- Telephone calls or letters. This is the most time-consuming way as it involves physically contacting friends and relations. However, it can be well worth the effort and other people may start passing on the information for you too

- Email. This is a quick and efficient way to publicize your website as you can email the information to a group of people with a single email. Also, you can include your website's URL (its address on the World Wide Web) so that people can access it directly from the email. To do this, open up your website and in the browser's address bar (the bar at the top of the browser that contains the URL) copy the URL and then write your email and paste the URL into it. This will become an active link for the recipients of the email

- Search engines. A lot of people find websites through search engines, such as Google or Yahoo! However, for your site to be found by a search engine you will have to register it with the relevant site. This can be done for individual sites, but a quicker way is to use a registration service that will send your site details to multiple search engines. For the basic service this should be free and one site that offers this is SubmitExpress at www. submitexpress.com:

2 Website nuts and bolts

At first sight a website can be a confusing collection of buttons, toolbars and varied content. This chapter looks at individual parts of a website to show how all of these elements make up the final site.

The role of the browser

A browser is an application that is used to display computer files. They can display a variety of different file formats, but most commonly they are used to display HTML web pages. The browser interprets the HTML code and then displays the content accordingly.

There are several different browsers available and they either come pre-installed on the computer or they can be downloaded from the company's website, usually for free. In some cases, browsers will interpret and display web pages slightly differently from each other, but in general they are all fairly consistent in the way they display pages. More complex web pages can cause inconsistencies in the way they are displayed, but simpler pages are usually displayed the same by different browsers.

The most commonly used browser is Internet Explorer but there are other browsers available, such as Firefox, Netscape Navigator and Apple's Safari for the Mac. All of these browsers serve a similar function of displaying web pages:

Internet Explorer

Don't forget

Internet Explorer comes pre-installed on Windows PCs. Safari comes pre-installed on Apple Mac computers running the operating system OS X.

Mozilla Firefox

Netscape Navigator

Don't forget

Firefox can be downloaded for free from www.mozilla.com/firefox/ Netscape Navigator can be downloaded for free at http://browser.netscape.com/ns8/

21

Apple Safari

Homepage

The homepage of a website is the first page you see when you access a site. In some ways it can be thought of as the index page; in a lot of cases the homepage is given the physical name of index.htm.

Since the homepage is your chance to make an impact with someone viewing your site for the first time, it is important that it is informative, pleasing on the eye and makes the user feel as if there is going to be something for them on the site.

There are some elements that should appear on the homepage:

- Introduction. This tells people about your site and what is on it

---

A fair exchange is a good bargain!

The Seniors Vacation And Home Exchange allows you to do a straight vacation exchange of your home. Or, if you prefer, exchange hospitality vacations. You visit with them and, in return, they visit with you.

Hot tip

The introduction on a homepage should appear clearly near the top of the page, be concise and tell people exactly what to expect on the site.

- Navigation. This is a collection of links that enables users to move to the other pages within your site

- Photographs. The subtle use of photographs can greatly enhance a homepage. However, do not have too many of them scattered around and keep them relatively small, so that they do not take over the whole page

There is no need to make a homepage overly complicated or containing too many "bells and whistles". Remember, you want people to keep coming back to your site, so what initially may seem like an eye-catching animation may just become irritating after it has been viewed half a dozen times. Keep your homepage clean and current so that it is welcoming, but not too overpowering.

Home button

When people are using your site you want to make sure that they never feel lost as they navigate their way through different pages. One way to achieve this is to make sure that there is a button, or a link, to the homepage on every page of your site. This means that wherever people are on the site they know that they can always quickly get back to the homepage. A homepage link can either be a textual link or a graphical one, but if you use a graphic, make sure that it is clearly labeled so that people know what it is.

The homepage button can appear anywhere at the top of a page. Traditionally, a homepage button is displayed at the top left corner of a page:

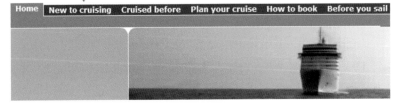

When users move to subsequent pages, the homepage button should be visible in the same place each time. However, the appearance of the homepage button, i.e. the color, can be changed to illustrate that you are no longer on the actual homepage.

Beware

If a home button is contained in a graphic and does not have an ALT tag (the small text box that appears when the cursor is passed over the graphic), users may not know that it can be used to access the homepage.

Additional pages

Some websites consist of a single page, but the majority have a number of subsequent pages that can be viewed by clicking on links on the homepage.

Hot tip

Using the same overall design, but changing photographs on additional pages, is a good way to show people that they have moved to a new page but are still within the same site.

Linked pages within a site should have the same look and feel as each other, so that users know that they are definitely still within the same site. Also, the navigation bar of links to other pages should appear in the same place on each page. This way, users will know exactly where to click to move to different pages.

You can have as many linked pages as you like on your website, but if you have too many then the users may be overwhelmed by the amount of information on your site.

Types of text

Text is an essential part of any website as it is used to convey the bulk of the information on the site. Text can be used in several ways on a site, to indicate different types of information.

Body text

This is the type of text that is used for the majority of the content of a web page. It should be large enough, so that it can be easily read, and there should be a good contrast between the text and the background. The font used for the body text should be consistent throughout the site.

Beware

Try to avoid using large blocks of unbroken body text, as this can be hard to read on a computer monitor. For more information about writing and displaying text on the Web, see Chapter 3.

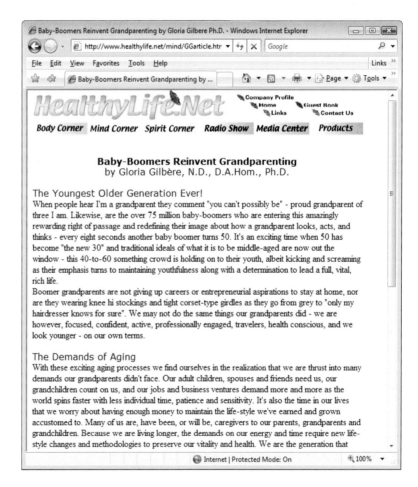

Headings

These are used to introduce the main topics on a page. Generally, there is one main heading per page. Headings should be created in the same font, size and color on every page on which they appear.

Sub-headings

These are used to break up the body text and highlight certain topics or types of information. As with main headings, they should be created consistently throughout the whole site.

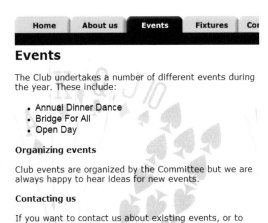

Hyperlinks

These are the links that can be clicked on to move to another part of the site. They can be graphical buttons or plain text. If they are text, they are frequently colored blue and underlined (see page 30).

(see page 30)

Don't forget

As web design has become more sophisticated, so the appearance of hyperlinks has changed. A lot of them are now rollovers, where the text changes appearance when the cursor passes over it.

27

Navigation bars

Navigation on a website refers to the process of moving from one point, on the site, to another. This can be to another page or it can be to another part of the same page. This is done through the use of hyperlinks (or just links), that enable the user to click on them and move to the linked item or page.

For the main areas of a website, i.e. the first pages that include new topics, it is a good idea to have links to these pages in an easily accessible group. This group of links is known as a navigation bar. This is usually displayed along the top or down the side of the page:

Ideally, the navigation bar should appear at the same place on every page of your website. This means that when you move to another page the navigation bar is still in the same position. This consistency gives the user the confidence to know that they will be able to navigate around the site from any page. In some cases the active page in a site, i.e. the one that is currently being viewed, will be highlighted in the navigation bar. This can be done by displaying the link for the current page in a different color from the other links:

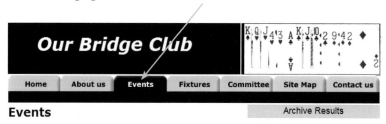

Photographs

Photographs are another important part of a website. Everyone likes to look at photos and they add a significant impact to any website. A plain text site can sometimes look less than inspiring:

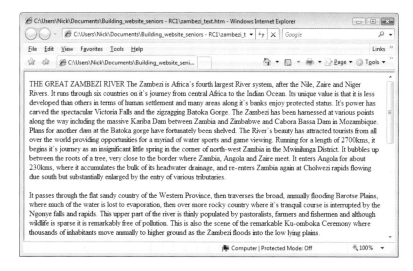

The inclusion of photographs give a website an immediate visual impact:

Beware

Never use photographs from other websites on your own site, unless you have first obtained permission.

Hyperlinks

Hyperlinks, also sometimes just called links, are the device on web pages that enable users to move from one part of a site to another. Hyperlinks can be within a single site and they can also be used to move to other sites on the World Wide Web. A hyperlink contains an instruction to the browser to open a particular web page, or to go to a specific location within a page. There are a number of ways in which links can be created:

Text links

A piece of text can be turned into a link, in which case it will frequently appear blue and be underlined:

Creating a site

- General

Once the link has been activated, the link will probably change color to show that it has been used:

Creating a site

- General

Graphical links

This is where graphical images are used to contain the link information, frequently as a button within a navigation bar:

Rollover links

This is where two graphical images are used to create a more sophisticated type of link.

When the cursor is rolled over the first image, the second one then appears:

By clicking on the image the link is activated.

Site map

One of the most important aspect of a website is to ensure that the person viewing always knows what is on the site, and how to get to each individual page. This is where a site map can prove invaluable. A site map is usually a single page that contains details of all of the different parts of the site. It also contains links to every listed page.

Site maps can be created in two ways; as an alphabetical index or as an expansion of the main navigation system.

Alphabetical site map

An alphabetical site map is a list of all of the pages within the site, arranged alphabetically. If there are a lot of pages, there can be an a-z list at the top of the page, allowing users to click on a letter and move to that specific section.

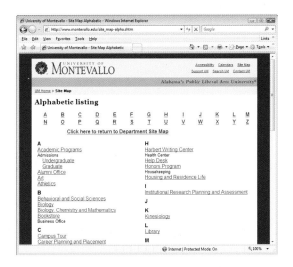

A page can then be selected, by clicking on the link, and this will take the user to the relevant page within the site.

Hot tip

Include a link to the site map in the main navigation bar. This way, users will always be able to access the site map in one click from any page they are on. They can then access any other page on the site in one click too, as long as all of the pages are listed on the site map.

Navigation site map

A navigation site map is one that mirrors the main navigation of the site, i.e. the links that are included in the navigation bar. However, the site map does not just list the top level navigation areas, it also shows the individual pages that are within that area. This way, the user can see exactly what is contained in each area.

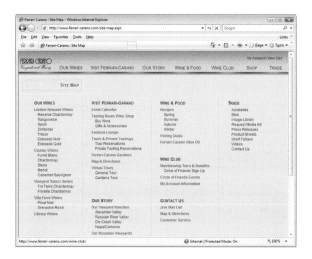

As with an alphabetical site map, the links within a navigation site map also take the user to the relevant page within the site.

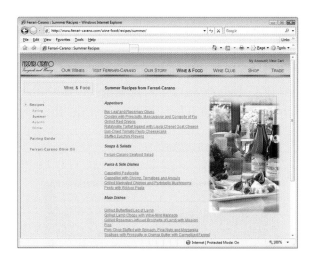

3 Good web design

Websites are all about conveying information and the design of a site can help greatly in this respect. This chapter deals with some of the issues to consider when designing an effective website.

Writing for the Web

It seems obvious to say, but the Web is a very different medium from paper-based media. One of the biggest differences for the users is that it is harder to read text on a computer monitor than a sheet of paper. This is primarily due to the glare from a monitor which can become very tiring on the eyes, even after a short period of time. Despite this, a lot of people who create content for websites do not take this into consideration and just reproduce hard copy information for an online environment. This is a big mistake and these types of websites will have people quickly clicking onto other sites.

When building websites, as much attention should be paid to the creation and presentation of the text on a site as there is to the overall design. Writing for the Web is a skill that has to be learned like any other but it is one that will be appreciated greatly by your audience.

Some statistics

- 79% of users always scan a web page; only 21% read word-for-word

- Reading from a monitor is 25% slower than from paper

- Web pages should be 50% smaller in terms of word count than the paper original

Think electronically

When you are operating in an online environment, you have to start thinking electronically, rather than the paper culture with which most people have grown up. Some points to consider when writing for the Web:

- Don't just reproduce hard copy electronically. Be prepared to drastically alter any hard copy text that you have and want to include on your website. Edit the text ruthlessly before it is included on the website and try and make it as concise and as punchy as possible. Look at websites that you like, or do not like, and then tailor your own content accordingly

- Create a visual road map. This can be used to guide people through your page, by signposting certain types of content. (See pages 36–37 for details)

- Dealing with long documents. Long documents (such as an extended family history) on a website can be fraught with danger: if they are reproduced as a single web page, it can create a daunting expanse of text and necessitate the person viewing it, having to perform a lot of scrolling to read the whole document. If necessary, break up long documents into smaller sections and create them as individual pages, that are all linked together

- Keep sentences short, concise and punchy. Check your own prose and also that of anyone else who is creating content for your site

- Use one idea per paragraph, even if it is a single sentence. This will help users follow the narrative of the text without too much effort

- Make sure your prose is straightforward and functional. Generally on the Web, people are looking for information rather than ground-breaking literary prose. Give them the information that they want or need and leave the purple prose to novelists

- Use short words rather than longer ones: remove all jargon where possible: certain acronyms and terminology may be very clear to you but this will not be the case for everyone. This is particularly true if you are involved with a hobby or a club website

- Print out your web pages and read them out loud to see if they still make sense. This is useful as a general proofreading exercise and also to check web specific items such as hyperlinks

- Print out your web pages to see how they appear. This will enable you to adjust them, if necessary, so that other users can also print them out. This is still favored by some users as they find it easier to read text this way

Hot tip

As a general rule, limit each page to just over a single monitor screen worth of text. But remember, some people may be viewing your site on a smaller, or bigger, monitor than your own.

Creating a roadmap

When we want to travel somewhere new, we frequently consult a map to find out where we are going, and how to get there. Similarly, with a web page it is vital to include some directions and signs to help new users find their way around the site. Even with text, it is possible to create a visual roadmap to help guide people through your site. Some ways in which this can be done are:

- Start with the conclusion first, so users don't have to read the whole page if they don't want to

- Highlight key words and phrases – use bold or colored text for highlighting

- Avoid hyperlinks containing "web terms" i.e. "click here", or, "Follow this link". Use hyperlinks to contain meaningful information too

- Use meaningful headings that convey relevant, specific information – avoid humor or puns (not everyone will share your sense of humor)

- Include bulleted and numbered lists. This helps to break up large blocks of text and creates white space

- Add quotes. These can be included in their own box on the page (known as pull quotes)

- Sidebars. These are parts of the text that are removed from the main body and presented separately, usually in the side margin. The text can also be enlarged for added emphasis

- Images. The use of small images within text is an excellent way to break it up and give it additional appeal

- Next Page and Previous Page links. These should be used to enable the user to navigate between sections of text that have been split into separate pages

- Breadcrumb trail. This is a set of links at the top of the page that shows the path that has been taken through the website to the current page

Hot tip

Look at newspapers and magazines to see how they break up text. Although this is different from presenting information on a website, it can still be a useful source of some general ideas.

Poor format

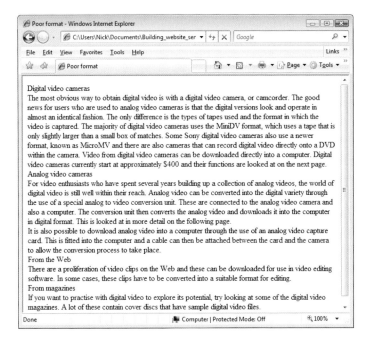

Beware

Writing and presenting effective textual content on a website can be a time-consuming process. However, it will be well worth it in the long run.

Good format

Including white space

With any type of written material, whether it is a book, a newspaper or a magazine, it can be difficult to read the text if it is packed too closely together. This is particularly true of web pages, as it is more tiring on the eyes to read from the screen than from paper. Because of this, it is important to actively include areas of white space when you are designing your web pages. White space on a website is not wasted space and it can be one of the best devices for producing a crisp, clean and attractive website. Some points to consider:

- Actively include white space, don't just let it happen

- Use white space, and also colored areas, to create an overall design

- White space can be used behind any part of a web page; text, images or hyperlinks

Use white space to break up your pages and highlight certain areas:

38

Less is more

For anyone new to building a website, the initial temptation can sometimes be to include everything they can on the site: numerous different fonts, bright colors, scrolling text, animations and almost anything else that they can create and publish successfully. However, this is frequently a mistake, and the maxim "less is more" is a very valuable one when building a website. The problem with overly designed sites is that they can look confusing and intimidating to new users, who might not know where to start:

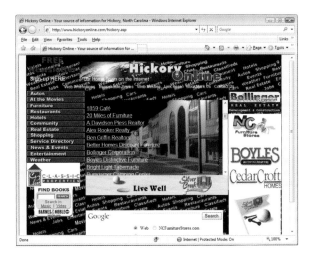

Beware

Websites that initially look very bold and striking can become irritating, once they have been viewed several times by users.

39

If a simpler, cleaner approach is adopted, the site will look a lot more welcoming and, it will be a lot easier to see what the site is for and how to use it:

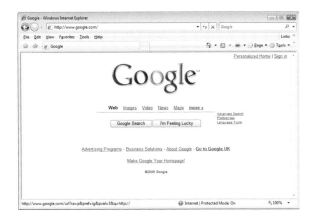

Using images

Images are a vital part of any website. If used properly they can add a stylish and effective element to your website. However, there are some issues to bear in mind when using images on a website:

- Make sure that the physical size of the image is not too large on the page, otherwise it could become too dominant and other information will be over-shadowed

- Use images with a small file size so that they do not take too long to download when the page is being viewed in a browser

- Do not use too many images on a page. One or two is usually enough, otherwise their impact will be lost

In general, images serve two main purposes on a website:

Don't forget

For more information on using and sharing images on websites, see Chapter 8.

1. They enhance the overall look of a page by breaking up the text and making it visually more appealing

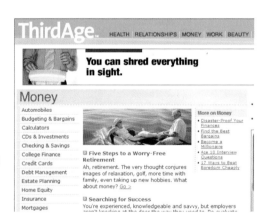

2. They can be used to represent a subject that is being covered on the page, or being linked to on another page

Five Steps to a Worry-Free Retirement

Ah, retirement. The very thought conjures images of relaxation, golf, more time with family, even taking up new hobbies. What about money? Go >

Dealing with multimedia

The World Wide Web has moved on dramatically from its early days of plain, static text, with no images (although at the time this was considered revolutionary itself). Web pages are now filled with a variety of multimedia content including:

- Audio

- Video

- Animation

Although multimedia can be very effective when done well it can be a complex area for those that are not familiar with it. Some points to consider:

- For a lot of multimedia, special programs (known as plug-ins) are required to display the content

Don't forget

One of the most common types of multimedia that you will come across on the Web is called Flash. This is a format for creating rich content animated sites and it requires the Flash Player to be installed to view this type of content.

- A lot of newer browsers include the most popular plug-ins for displaying multimedia content. However, a lot of older versions do not

- Multimedia content can take a lot longer to download than static text. Therefore, for users with a slow Internet connection, the process of viewing multimedia may be a frustrating one

- From a website building point of view, it is more complex to include multimedia on a site

Increasing text size

If your website and its pages are not appealing to visitors, it is unlikely that they will stay for too long. If they do, they may find the experience frustrating and unfulfilling. A number of design elements can be used to make a page easier on the eye and one of the most important is the amount of text on a page and its size. If a page has a lot of densely packed, small, text it is unlikely that people will spend too long trying to read it.

Why text size matters

1 A small text size can make a page look too intimidating and visitors may not want to give themselves eye strain by trying to read all of it

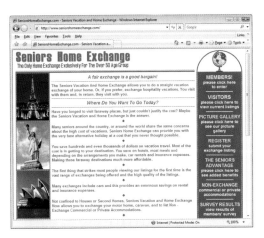

2 A larger text size makes a page instantly more appealing, with the result that visitors are more likely to spend time there

... cont'd

Changing the text size

When building a website it is possible to specify the size of the text on a page. However, as a user it is also possible to change the size of text while you are viewing a web page through a browser. To do this:

1 Open a web page and assess whether the text is the right size or not

2 In Internet Explorer, select View>Text Size from the Menu bar and select an appropriate text size from the options

3 The text will be displayed at the selected size. Depending on how the page has been designed, some elements may appear at their original size

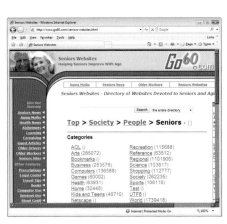

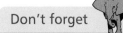

Don't forget

Web browsers change the text size by using slightly different processes. For Mozilla Firefox the command is View>Text Size> Increase/Decrease. For Safari (Mac users) the command is View> Make Text Bigger/Make Text Smaller.

43

...cont'd

Adding text size instructions

When you discover how to change the size of the text on a web page, you can then incorporate this into your own website: there is no point in keeping this to yourself.

Including information about changing text size is an excellent option for your own website. This is because it shows visitors that you are thinking about them, and their needs, and you have gone to the trouble to try and make their visit to your website as enjoyable as possible.

To include details about changing text size on your website:

1. On your homepage, include a link that is titled Text size (or something similar). This will link to a separate page that contains information about changing the text size

Text size

2. Create a linked page that contains the information for changing text size. Make this as clear as possible and include the same information for the most commonly used browsers

Accessibility

The issue of accessibility is one that is concerned with providing as many people as possible with access to websites, regardless of any disabilities they may have. When creating something for the public domain, such as a website, it is essential to try and include as wide a range of users as possible. Accessibility is a huge issue, but some points to consider are:

- Consider all types of disability: blind or partially sighted, deaf, limited motor skills (i.e. users who find it difficult to operate a mouse), dyslexia, learning difficulties etc.

- Blind or partially sighted users use access readers that read the text on a web page. This has implications for page design as the readers may not view a web page in the same way as a sighted person. Remember also, that older people generally have poorer eyesight and so will require the text on a website to be larger

- Always label images with ALT (alternative) tags. These are textual tags that appear if a browser is set to not display images and also when the cursor is passed over an image (see below)

- Do not include core information in images, i.e. textual information in images. If you do, make sure that there is also a plain text alternative

- Be careful with any type of multimedia content, such as animations, video or content created with Flash software. This can be hard for some users with disabilities to view satisfactorily

Don't forget

For an in-depth look at accessibility issues, look at the Web Accessibility Initiative (WAI) at: www.w3.org/WAI/

Top ten design tips

Building your own website is an enjoyable and educational process. In order to get the most out of it, here are some design tips to follow:

- Know your audience. You know best who you are building your website for and you should create it accordingly. Generally, design a site that you would like to see yourself

- Keep it simple. Sometimes websites are created for the benefit of the designer, rather than for the benefit of the users. The users should always be at the forefront of anyone designing a website

- White space. Use white space creatively and specifically to create areas within a page that break up the rest of the content

- Create for online. Remember that you are operating in an online environment and create your content accordingly: cut down on the amount of text and present this for an online audience

- Use small photographs

- Straightforward and consistent navigation. Select a navigation system that is logical and appears at the same place on every page

- Use a site map. List all of the pages on your site within a site map. This will enable users to move quickly anywhere within the site

- Know your limitations. If you don't feel confident with something then don't do it

- Develop your skills. Once you are more confident, experiment with new techniques. However, always make sure that this is offline initially, i.e. not your live site

- Check your site before it is published. Always check everything on your site before it is published and becomes live. Better to discover mistakes at this stage

Don't forget

A simple website does not have to be boring. If it is well designed and thought out, then it can be stylish and effective but at the same time subtle and unobtrusive.

4 Using GeoCities

GeoCities is a hugely popular online service for creating family, hobby and club websites. This chapter introduces GeoCities and shows how you can soon have your first page on the Web.

What GeoCities does

GeoCities is an online website publishing service. It operates by giving users an online environment (i.e. its own website) in which to build and publish websites. This means that people do not have to first create web pages on their own computers and then copy them onto the computers of a web hosting service: GeoCities does it all in one location.

GeoCities is aimed primarily at people who want to be able to publish and edit web pages but, who are not concerned with HTML and the technical aspect of creating the pages. It is an ideal service for family, hobby, club or charity websites. There are a number of service offered by GeoCities, but the basic web building service is free.

With GeoCities you can make the web building process as easy or as complicated as you like.

48

Hot tip

A single web page can be published in a matter of a few minutes using GeoCities PageWizards.

There are a variety of tools for building websites. Some, such as the PageWizards, offer a simple step-by-step approach:

Other tools, such as PageBuilder give you more control over the layout and design of your page:

No need for HTML

Although you can create your own pages in HTML and then publish them on an online site, there is absolutely no necessity to know anything about HTML. Online services use a variety of templates and wizards to create the page designs and styles:

Don't forget

It is a good idea to have a general understanding of HTML when you are building websites. For more information about this have a look at "HTML in Easy Steps" in this series.

49

All you have to do is add the textual content and select the images that you want to insert into the templates. However, this is not to say that there is no HTML created when you build your website with an online service. The normal code is created in the background (see below) and this looks the same as if it had been created manually. Luckily, you do not have to have anything to do with this if you do not want to.

Getting registered

Before you can start building a website on GeoCities, you first have to be registered. This is free to do and only takes a few minutes. To do this:

1 Access the GeoCities homepage at http://geocities.yahoo.com/

2 Click the Sign Up Now button to start the registration process

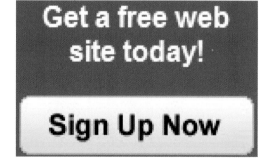

3 You will be taken to the login/registration page

4 To register, click the Sign Up link

To access Yahoo! GeoCities...

Don't have a Yahoo! ID?
Signing up is easy.

Sign Up

5 Enter your registration details. These include your name, Yahoo! ID and password

Beware

Do not disclose your registration details to anyone. If you do, they would be able to access your GeoCities account and change your site without you knowing about it.

6 Click on the Submit This Form Securely button

Submit This Form Securely

7 Once you have completed the registration process, you will see the Welcome window that contains details about your registration. Click here to continue

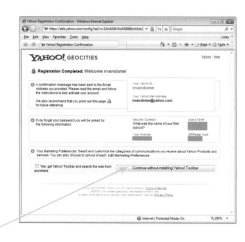

8 Select details here about the type of site that you want to build (this is for information only and not binding), and how you heard about GeoCities

9 To ensure that the registration is not an automated one, a code will be displayed here. Enter this in the box provided

10 Click on the Submit button to leave the registration area and start building your website

Getting started with Wizards

Once you have registered with Yahoo! GeoCities you can start building your first website. The beauty of this method is that you can have a site up and running on the World Wide Web within a matter of minutes. The quickest way to do this is by using the GeoCities PageWizards. To do this:

1 Once you have left the registration area, click on the Build your web site now link; or

Your Yahoo! ID and Home Page Information	
Your Yahoo! ID is:	nvandome
Your home page URL shortcut is:	http://www.geocities.com/nvandome

Build your web site now!

2 When you next return to the GeoCities homepage, click on the Sign in to GeoCities link

Are you already a GeoCities user?

▶ Sign in to GeoCities

3 Enter your Yahoo! ID and password (these will have been created during the registration process)

Sign in to Yahoo!

Prevent Password Theft

Yahoo! ID: nvandome

Password: ••••••••

☐ Remember my ID on this computer

Sign In

4 Click the Sign In button

Don't forget

Once you have registered with GeoCities your Yahoo! ID will be used as part of your homepage address within the site, e.g. http://geocities.com/myid

53

...cont'd

5 Once you have logged in, you will see a page that contains all of the website building options within GeoCities. This is known as the Control Panel

6 The Getting Started section contains help details, as well as website building tools

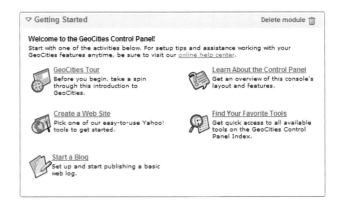

7 Click the Create a Web Site link to access options for building your site

...cont'd

8 The Control Panel now displays the two main options for building a website: PageBuilder and PageWizards. Of the two, PageBuilder is more advanced, so for an initial web page PageWizards is the best choice

Don't forget

PageWizards consists of templates for the design of the page. Once content is added this is automatically inserted into the template design.

55

9 Under the Yahoo! PageWizards section, click on the Try PageWizards link

→ **The Quickest Web Page Yahoo! PageWizards**
For simplicity and speed.

- Create a page in four easy steps
- Get guided help building your page
- Choose from more than a dozen templates

Try PageWizards

Selecting a template

Once the PageWizards has been accessed, the first step is to select a template. This is a preset design into which your page content can then be added. To do this:

1 The main templates are displayed here

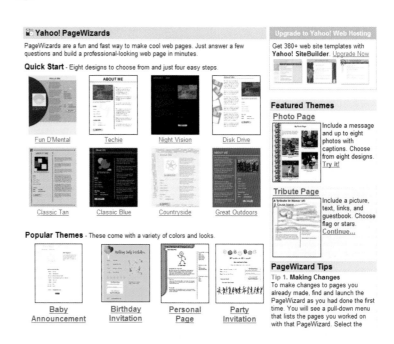

Hot tip

Once you have selected a template, it is still possible to change it at a later time, either during the current PageWizards, or even a different editing session.

2 To select a template, click the link underneath the graphic

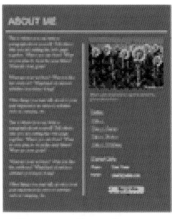

Great Outdoors

3 The Welcome page describes the process of creating a web page with PageWizards

4 Click the Begin button to start the Wizard

5 At this stage you still have the chance to select another template. Check on the button next to the template name to select it

6 Click the Next button to move to the next step of the Wizard

Adding text and images

Text and images are an integral part of any website, and they can both easily be added with the PageWizards. To do this:

 On the next page of the Wizard, enter a title for the page here

Enter text for the page here

Click the Next button to move to the next step of the Wizard

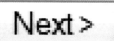

In the next window you have the choice of adding a photograph of your own or one chosen by the template

Click the Upload new image button to select a photograph from your own computer

Upload new image...

Hot tip

It is always better to include your own photographs rather than the default ones, if possible.

6 Click the Browse button

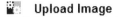

Upload Image

Click the Browse button to select your image.

Browse...

Upload

7 Locate the photo that you want and click the Open button

59

8 The filepath of the image is added in the Upload Image window.

Upload Image

Click the Browse button to select your image.

C:\Users\Nick\Documer Browse...

Upload

Click the Upload button to have the image uploaded into the PageWizards template

9 The image name is now displayed within the PageWizards

❷ Pick your picture

◉ Use your own image

Pick from your account

sunflowers.jpg ▼ - preview image

Final touches and publishing

Once the main content has been added in the PageWizards, the finishing touches can be applied before the page is published. To do this:

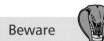

60

1 On the next page of the Wizard, enter links to other web pages here

2 Click the Next button to move to the next step of the Wizard

3 In the next window enter your own details, such as your email address, for people who want to get in contact with you

4 Click the Next button to move to the next step of the Wizard

Next >

5 Enter a name for your page. This will be used as part of the page's URL (web address)

6 Click the Next button to move to the next step of the Wizard

Don't forget

The web address of a page is the location on the World Wide Web, at which it can be viewed in a browser.

7 The page has now been created and its web address is shown here

8 Click the Done button to complete the PageWizards

Viewing your page

Once your page has been published, there are two ways to view it on the World Wide Web:

 Click on this link in the PageWizards; or

View the Page

You can bookmark this URL or send it to friends.

http://www.geocities.com/nvandome/sunflowers.html

 Copy the whole of the web address and paste it into the address bar of a web browser

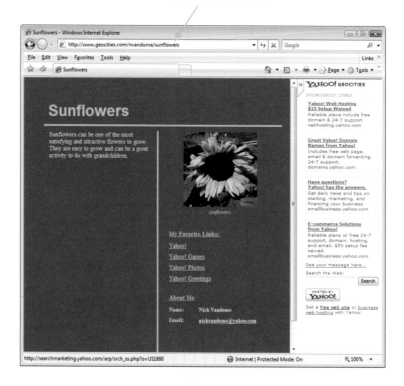

The completed page can then be viewed as it will appear to anyone looking at it on the Web

Editing a page

After you have published your first web page, and told everyone about it, you can then sit back and relax and enjoy the fact that you now have a physical presence on the World Wide Web. However, this does not mean that you can get complacent and never pay any attention to your page again: websites that are not edited and refreshed on a regular basis are doomed to failure as people will become bored quickly with looking at exactly the same content. Therefore, it is important that you update your page as often as you can, within reason. Using the PageWizards it is possible to edit some, or all, of your page. To do this:

1. Access the GeoCities homepage and click on the Sign in to GeoCities link

   Are you already a GeoCities user?

   ▶ **Sign in to GeoCities**

2. Enter your Yahoo! ID and password and click the Sign In button

   Already have a Yahoo! ID?
   Sign in.

   Yahoo! ID: nvandome

   Password: •••••••

   ☐ Remember my ID on this computer

   Sign In

3. In the GeoCities Control Panel, click the Create & Update tab

   GeoCities Control Panel

   | Home | Create & Update | Manage |

4. Click the Yahoo! Page-Wizards link

   Yahoo! PageWizards

   For a quick start, use this Yahoo! click-and-build wizard to create a simple home page.

Don't forget

Pages can also be edited by returning directly to the PageWizards, in the same way as you accessed it for the first time.

5 Select a template design from within the PageWizards (this can be the same as for your published page or a different one). Click on the link underneath the design

Great Outdoors

6 Click this button on to edit an existing page

7 Select the page to be edited from the drop down list here. Click on the Next button

8 Make editing changes to the page in the same way as for creating the page originally. Click on the Next button to move through the PageWizards

9 If you cancel the editing session before you have gone through the whole PageWizards, the changes will not be applied

5 Using PageBuilder

Another option for building websites within GeoCities is PageBuilder, which gives you more control over the overall design. This chapter shows you how to get started with creating pages in PageBuilder.

Accessing PageBuilder

For website builders on GeoCities who want to take a bit more control over their design once they have mastered the PageWizards, the PageBuilder option is an excellent way. The PageBuilder is a facility that allows users to design their own pages, without the limitations of a pre-designed template. As with the PageWizards though, all of the HTML is still created automatically in the background.

To use PageBuilder you have to first launch the program within GeoCities itself. To do this:

 1 Access the GeoCities homepage and click the Sign in to GeoCities link

Are you already a GeoCities user?

 Sign in to GeoCities

Beware

Once PageBuilder has been launched and is running, there will be an open window that is needed for PageBuilder to operate properly. Make sure that you do not close this window.

2 Enter your Yahoo! ID and password then click the Sign In button

Already have a Yahoo! ID?
Sign in.

Yahoo! ID: nvandome

Password: ••••••••

☐ Remember my ID on this computer

Sign In

3 In the GeoCities Control Panel, click the Create a Web Site link

Create a Web Site
Pick one of our easy-to-use Yahoo! tools to get started.

4 On the next page click the Try PageBuilder link

▷ **Point-and-Click Power**
Yahoo! PageBuilder
For a personalized web site.

Widget Designs, Inc.

• Express yourself with completely customizable pages
• Personalize with pictures, special effects, and more
• Create pages fast with drag-and-drop editing

Try PageBuilder

5 To launch PageBuilder, click the Launch PageBuilder box

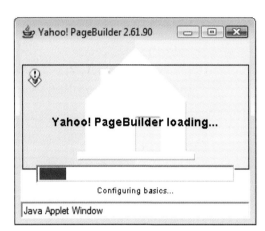

6 The following window appears while PageBuilder is loading

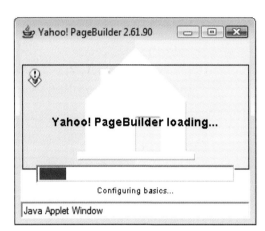

7 Once Page-Builder is loaded, it is ready for use to start building web pages

Opening existing pages

PageBuilder can be used to create web pages from scratch and it can also be used to open and edit existing pages, regardless of where the pages were first created. To do this:

Don't forget

Each time that you log out of GeoCities, you will have to relaunch PageBuilder whenever you want to use it again.

Beware

If you have created a page in the PageWizards and then open and save it in PageBuilder, you will then not be able to open it in the PageWizards again.

1 On the PageBuilder toolbar, click the Open button

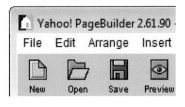

2 Select the page that you want to open and click the Open button

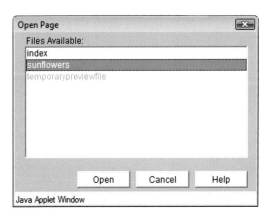

3 The selected page is opened within the PageBuilder window, ready for editing

Opening a new page

If you want to create your own web pages from scratch, PageBuilder provides an ideal environment to do this. Initially, you have to open a blank page. To do this:

1   On the PageBuilder toolbar, click the New button

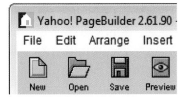

2   A new, blank page is opened within the PageBuilder window. Content can now be added to the page

Adding text

The first thing that you will probably want to add to a new page is text. This can be in the form of a heading, sub-heading or the body text of the page that tells people about it. To add text:

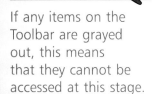

Hot tip

If any items on the Toolbar are grayed out, this means that they cannot be accessed at this stage.

 Options for all of the main functions within PageBuilder are located in the Toolbar at the top of the PageBuilder window

Click on this button to select the Text tool

A text box is automatically inserted in the center of the current page

Start typing to add text

5 To move a text box, click and hold on to the border of the box and drag it around the page to the desired position

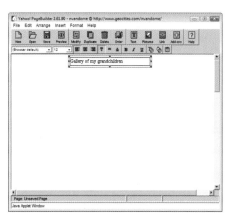

6 To change the font, click here and select a new font from the visible list

7 To change the size of the text, click here and select a new size from the visible list

8 If the text goes onto another line, drag one of the side resizing points to display it on a single line again

Gallery of my grandchildren

71

Formatting text

Plain text on a website can begin to look a little mundane if there is too much of it, so it is important to be able to format text in terms of position and appearance. To do this:

1 Underneath the main Toolbar, use these buttons to position text horizontally and vertically

Left and top aligned

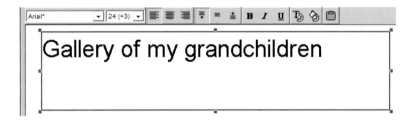

Center and middle aligned

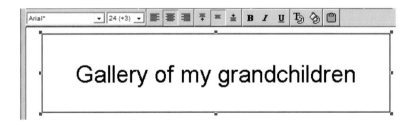

Right and bottom aligned

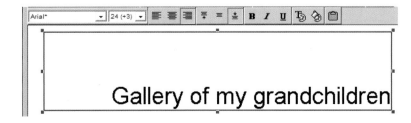

Changing color

To change the color of a piece of text:

1 Select the text on the page by dragging the cursor over it in the text box

Don't forget

Always ensure that there is a good contrast between the text color and the background color.

2 Click this button on the Toolbar

3 Select a color from the color chart and click the OK button

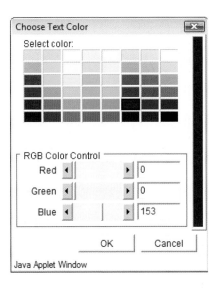

4 The selected color is applied to the text

Gallery of my grandchildren

73

Bold, italics and underlining

Bold, italics and underling are all ways of giving text more emphasis. To do this:

  Underneath the main Toolbar, use these buttons to apply bold (B), italics (I) and underlining (U)

Bold text

Italic text

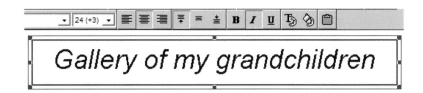

Beware

Try not to use underlined text on a website, as this is usually associated with a hyperlink to another page or website on the Web.

Underlined text

Adding images

Text is excellent for conveying information on a website, but images are essential to give the design a more eye-catching appearance. In PageBuilder, images can be added from either a clip art collection from within GeoCities, or you can use your own images.

Using clip art images

1 Click on button on the Toolbar

2 The options for selecting images are displayed in the Select Picture window

3 Double-click on Clipart to view the sub-categories

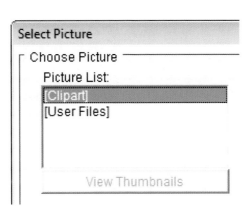

Beware

Clip art images should be used sparingly on a web page, as too many of them can make a page look too jokey and childish.

...cont'd

Don't forget

Keep double-clicking on the sub-categories until the images themselves are listed. You will be able to tell this because they will have a .gif extension.

④ Double-click a sub-category to see the available images

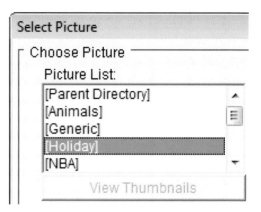

⑤ Click an image to view it in the Preview box

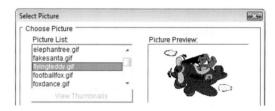

⑥ If you want to include the image on your page, click the OK button

OK

⑦ The image is inserted onto the page

Using your own images

Using your own images on your website gives you a lot more flexibility and makes it a lot more personal. To do this:

1 In the Select Picture window, click the Upload button in the Upload Your Own Picture section

Upload Your Own Picture

Click Upload to add a picture from your computer   Upload...

2 The next window has options for selecting and uploading your own images

3 Click the Browse button to find images on your own computer

4 Browse to the required images on your computer and select one

77

...cont'd

5 Click the Open button to add the selected image

6 Repeat the process for all of the images that you want to include on your website

7 Click the Upload button to copy the images from your computer onto GeoCities

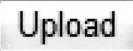

8 While the images are being uploaded, the following message is displayed

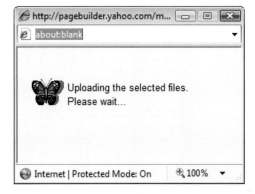

9 Once all of the images have been uploaded, they are displayed in the Upload Files window

10 Click the OK button if these are the files that you want to include

11 You will be returned to the Select Picture window. Double-click on the User Files in the Picture List box

Don't forget

Even once files have been uploaded, they still have to be selected from the Picture List, in order to add them to a page.

...cont'd

12 Select an image in the Picture List box. This will be displayed in the Picture Preview box

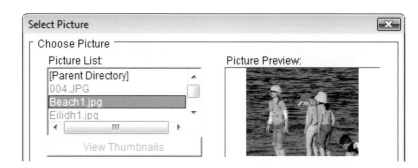

13 Click the OK button to add the image to your web page

14 The image is displayed on the page within PageBuilder

Moving images

When images are added to a PageBuilder page, there is no control over where they are inserted. However, it is easy to move them once they have been included. To do this:

1 Add more images in the same way as the process described on the previous pages. Images that overlap will be covered with red cross-hatching to indicate the overlap

2 Click and drag images to move them around the page until they are in the desired positions

Adding a background

Although a white background can be effective on a web page, there are times when a colored background can be beneficial, particularly if there are a lot of images on a page. To do this:

1 From the Menu bar select Insert>Basics> Background

2 The Background Properties window has options for adding various types of backgrounds to a page

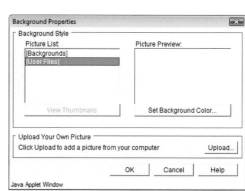

3 Click the Set Background Color button

Set Background Color...

4 Select a color and click the OK button. The exact details about the color are displayed in the RGB Color Control box

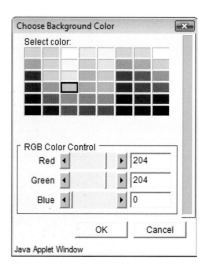

5 The selected color is displayed in the Picture Preview box, in the Background Properties window

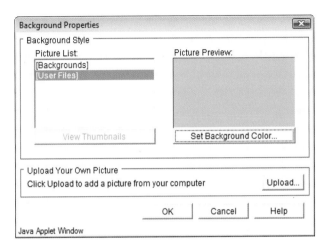

6 Click the OK button to apply the background color

OK

7 The color is applied as a background on the PageBuilder page

83

Previewing pages

Pages can be previewed at any time with PageBuilder and it is a good idea to do this frequently, so that you can see what your design looks like when it is viewed, within the GeoCities environment in a web browser. To preview a page:

1 Click this button on the Toolbar

2 The page is displayed as it will look once it is published. At this point it cannot be viewed by anyone else

Beware

If you are using the GeoCities free service, there will be a number of GeoCities advertisements at the side of your web pages, both when they are previewed and also when they are published.

Saving pages

Once you have built a page and previewed the content you can then save it. With PageBuilder the Save command also serves to publish the page. To save and publish a page:

1 Select File>Save from the Menu bar, or

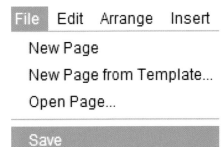

2 Click the Save button on the Toolbar

3 The name of the file to be saved is displayed here

Don't forget

If you want to save a different file that you have been working on, select it from the Files Available in the Save Page window and click on the Save button.

4 Click the Save button

5 Once the file has been saved and published, the following window is displayed

6 Click the OK button if you want to view your page

OK

7 The page is displayed as it appears on the World Wide Web

8 The web address of the page (URL) is displayed in the address bar of the browser displaying the page

6 More with PageBuilder

This chapter reveals the full power of PageBuilder and shows how it can be used to add a number of eye-catching and dynamic elements to your website to enhance its appeal.

Creating a homepage

A homepage is the default page that users see whenever your site address is entered into a web browser. Usually, homepages have the name "index.htm" or "index.html", as this is the name that browsers automatically look for when searching for a homepage.

So, if your site address on GeoCities is www.geocities.com/mysite, and this is entered into a browser it will display the homepage, i.e. www.geocities.com/mysite/index.html

When you first register with GeoCities an index page is automatically created for you. At this point the page has no content of your own and looks like this:

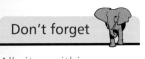

Don't forget

All sites within GeoCities have to have an index.html page.

To edit your homepage and add your own content, first open it in PageBuilder:

1 Select File> Open from the Menu bar and select the index file. Click the Open button to open the index file in PageBuilder

2 Select all of the current content on the page and delete it by pressing the Delete button on your keyboard

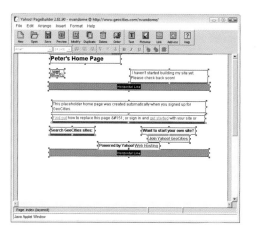

To select all elements on a page, hold down the Ctrl button on the keyboard and click on all of the elements.

3 The page will now be blank, ready for new content to be added

89

Beware

Remember to Save your page at regular intervals when you are adding new content.

4 Add text and images as shown in the previous chapter

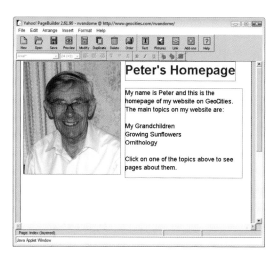

...cont'd

5 When you are happy with the content, click the Save button on the Toolbar

When a page is saved in PageBuilder, it is automatically published at the same time. This means that it is live on the Web and can be viewed by anyone with an Internet connection.

6 In the Save & Publish window, click the OK button

7 The homepage can then be viewed on the Web

Adding hyperlinks

Hyperlinks, frequently referred to as just links, are the devices used on the World Wide Web for moving from one place to another. This is done by clicking on a link. Links can be made within a single page, to other pages within the same site, other sites on the Web or to an email address. The most common type of links are those that connect the different pages of your own site. To do this you have to first create two or more separate pages. The pages can then be linked together. To do this:

1. On the first page, highlight the text that you want to make into the hyperlink

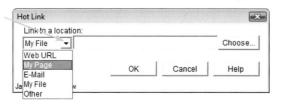

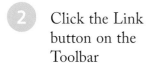

2. Click the Link button on the Toolbar

3. Click here and select the type of link that you want to create

4. Click the Choose button

Hot tip

Hyperlinks can also be made to other web pages (Web URL in the Hot Link window). To do this, you have to enter the full web address of the page to which you want to link, e.g. http://www.mypage.com

Hot tip

Hyperlinks can also be made to email addresses (E-mail in the Hot Link window). To do this you have to enter "mailto:" followed by the email address, e.g. mailto:me@yahoo.com

...cont'd

5   Select the file to which you want to link

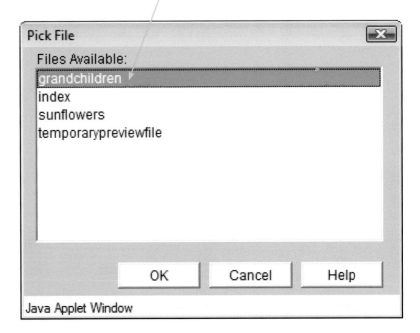

Hot tip

Only pages that you have created, and published, will be available for linking to if the My Page option is selected in the Hot Link window.

6   Click the OK button   **OK**

7   The type of link and the target page (i.e. the one to which the link will go) are both displayed in the Hot Link window

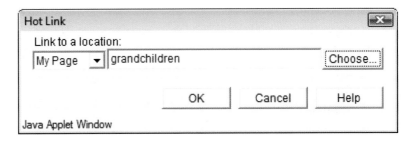

8   Click the OK button   

9 The selected text is converted into a link, which is indicated by the text turning blue and being underlined

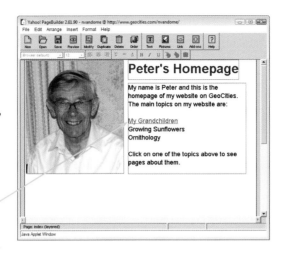

10 Once the page is saved and published, the link is active on the page on the Web. Click the link to activate it

Don't forget

Always check links once they have been created and published. Make sure that the correct page appears when the link is activated, i.e. clicked.

11 Once the link is activated, the linked page is opened

Adding lines

Horizontal lines are an excellent device for separating different types of content on a web page and also for adding a new graphical element to the page. To do this:

Hot tip

Horizontal lines are a good design feature for breaking up large amounts of text.

Don't forget

Other options in the Basics section include: adding music files, graphical buttons, vertical lines and a counter to show how many people have visited your site.

1 Click the Add-ons button on the Toolbar

2 Click the Basics section

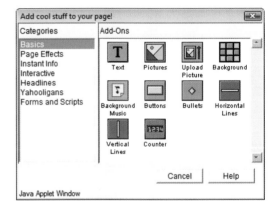

3 Click the Horizontal Lines button

4 Double-click the Horizontal Lines option to see the available types of lines

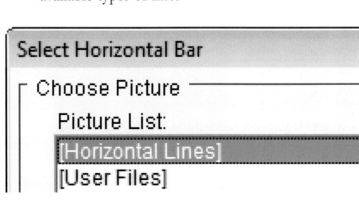

5 Click a type of line to view it in the Picture Preview window

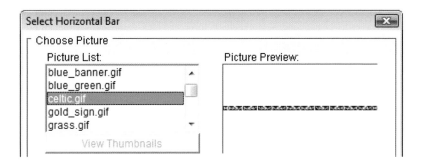

6 Click the OK button to add a particular line to your page

7 The line is added to the page and can be moved and resized in the same way as any other graphical element on the page

Don't forget

To resize a horizontal line, click on it to select it and then drag one of the resizing handles that appear around its border.

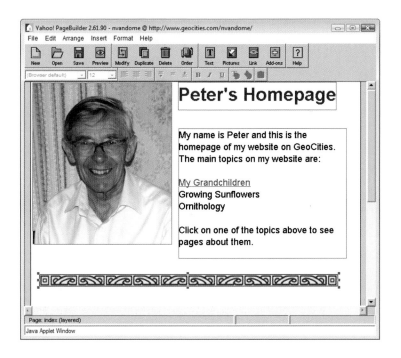

Adding a time stamp

A time stamp is a device for displaying the correct time on your site. It can also be used to display the current date. To do this:

1 Click the Add-ons button on the Toolbar

2 Click the Instant Info section

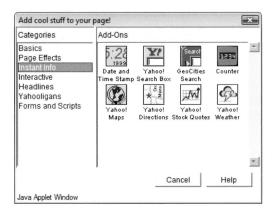

96

3 Click the Date and Time Stamp button

Date and
Time Stamp

4 Select the formatting options for the date and time stamp, i.e. the way it will appear on your web page

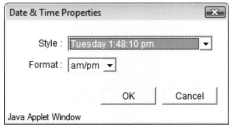

5 Click the OK button

OK

6 The Date and Time box can be positioned anywhere on your page by clicking on it and dragging it to the desired location

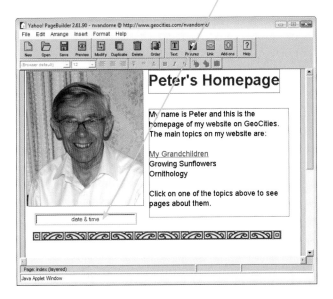

Hot tip

The format, for the way in which the date and time are displayed, can be edited by double-clicking on the Date and Time box and then selecting options from the subsequent window.

97

7 Once the page is saved and published, the Date and Time stamp becomes active

Adding a guestbook

Websites can really come to life when they become interactive and allow other people to contribute to them. One way of doing this is to add a guestbook to your site, so that family and friends can add comments about your site and give their own views. To do this:

1 Click the Add-ons button on the Toolbar

2 Click the Interactive section

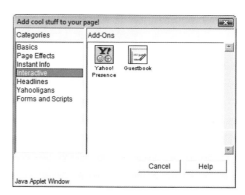

98

3 Click the Guestbook button

Guestbook

4 A Yahoo! Wizard takes you through the process of creating your guestbook

5 Click the Begin button

6 Enter a title for your guestbook and a description for what you want included in it. Click the Next button to continue

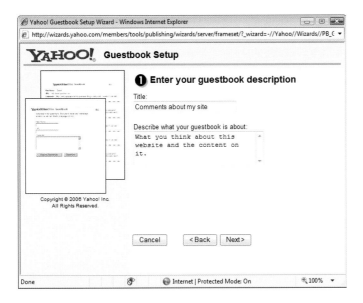

7 Select a color for the font and the background of the guestbook. Click the Next button to continue

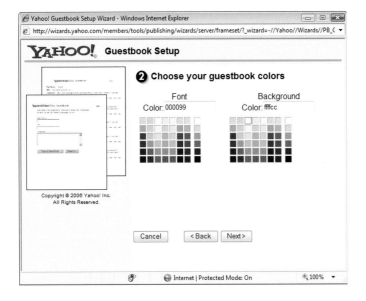

...cont'd

8 Select the type of information you want people to enter in the guestbook when they visit. Click the Next button to continue

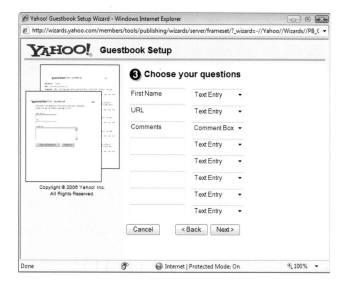

9 Select any formatting options such as how entries are displayed. Click the Next button to continue

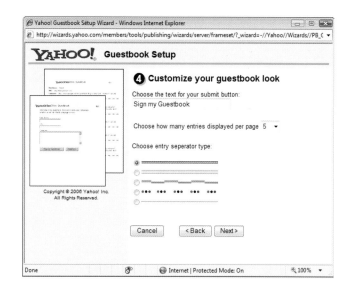

10 Select details for how you want to be notified when someone makes an entry in the guestbook. Click the Next button to continue

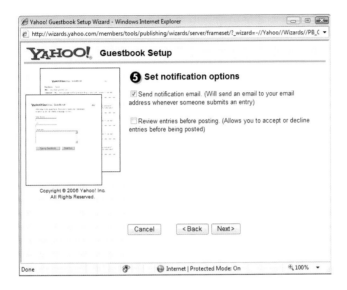

Don't forget

Notification of an entry in your guestbook is done by GeoCities sending you an automated email.

11 Click the Done button to complete setting up your guestbook

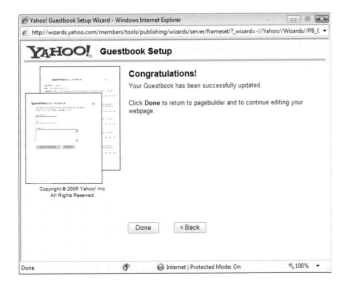

Using a guestbook

Once a guestbook has been added to a GeoCities page, it can then be added to or viewed once the page has been published. To do this:

1. To make an entry in a guestbook, click the Sign My GuestBook link on the homepage

Sign My GuestBook

2. Enter the details for your entry

What you think about this website and the content on it.

First Name

URL

Comments

Sign my Guestbook   Clear form

102

3. Click the Sign my Guestbook button

Sign my Guestbook

4. To view a guestbook, click the View My GuestBook link

View My GuestBook

5. The entries for the guestbook, and who they are from, are listed in order on a separate page

First Name : Nick
URL : nvandome@yahoo.com
Comments : Great website. Love the photos and the information about sunflowers.

Managing files

As well as creating new files, GeoCities also has a facility for viewing and managing the files that you have created or uploaded for your site. This is known as the File Manager, and enables you to delete unwanted files, upload new ones from your computer and other housekeeping tasks. To use File Manager from within PageBuilder:

1 Select File>File Manager from the Menu bar

2 Click the Pages tab to view the web pages that have been created (or uploaded from another source)

Hot tip

File Manager can also be accessed from the GeoCities Control Panel. To do this, click on the Manage button and select the File Manager link under the File Management Tools section.

3 Click the Images tab to view the images that have been uploaded for inclusion on your web pages

...cont'd

Creating a new folder

As you create more pages, and possibly different types of sites, it is useful to have different folders into which you can store files for separate projects. To create a new folder:

1 In File Manager, click the New Folder button

NewFolder

2 Enter a name for the new folder

3 Click the Create button

Create

4 You are notified that the folder has been created. Click the OK button

Folder Vacations **was created successfully**

OK

5 The new folder is displayed in File Manager and content can be added to it

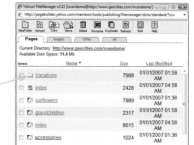

Other File Manager functions

File Manager can also be used for other general editing tasks. These are:

Upload

Upload. This can be used to copy files from your own computer to your GeoCities file structure. These files can then be used within your website.

Copy

Copy. This can be used to copy files within your file structure. This creates two versions of the same file but, you have to give the copy a different filename.

Move

Move. This can be used to move files from one folder, within your file structure, to another.

Delete

Delete. This can be used to remove files from within your file structure.

Rename

Rename. This can be used to change the name of a file.

Duplicate

Duplicate. This can be used to create a copy of a file in the current directory. However, the copy has to be given a different filename.

Exit

Exit. This can be used to exit from File Manager.

Help

Help. This contains help information about using File Manager.

Beware

If you rename a file, make sure that you change any links in your site that link to the file that has been renamed. Otherwise the links will not work.

105

Monitoring activity

When you are using GeoCities, the Control Panel contains windows that allow you to monitor various activities, including the amount of space that you have used up in your GeoCities account and, how many people have visited your site over certain periods.

Site Status

This contains information about how much data you have transferred onto GeoCities over a specific period of time (hourly) and how much storage space your files are taking up on GeoCities.

Don't forget

For the free GeoCities account, you are given 15 megabytes (Mb) of space for storing the files for your website. Unless you are uploading a lot of very large photographs, this should be plenty for most websites.

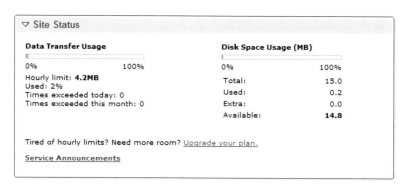

Site Activity

This contains information about the number of times that your pages have been viewed.

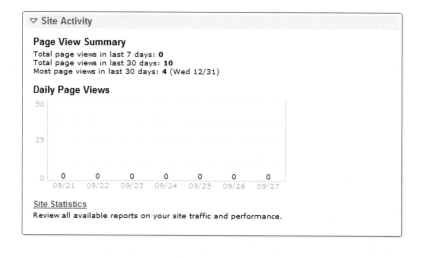

7 Building a family site

This chapter covers the type of information that can be included on a family website and shows how to research, compile and then display it on your site.

What to include

By its nature, a family website is individual to the people involved and no two family sites will be the same. Before you start your family site, it is a good idea to note down the members of the family who you think will be using the site the most. You can then start listing some of their interests and hobbies and build up some content ideas this way.

Some general areas of information that can be included on a family website are:

- Family history. This can be as short or as long as you like as this is an area that will undoubtedly generate a lot of interest among family members and hopefully, people will also contribute more information. If you are writing an extensive family history then remember to present it in a way that is easily viewed on the Web: break the information down into logical sections and make sure that there are plenty of headings, sub-headings, bullet points and sidebar information

- Family tree. A natural extension of a narrative family history is a graphical family tree. This is when all of the members of a family (or as many as you want to include or can find information about) are displayed in a connected chart. There are specific computer programs that can be used to produce family trees on the Web and they can also be created on a lot of genealogy sites

- Photo galleries. Pages containing photographs of family members are an excellent option for a family website, and this is one area that is most likely to keep people coming back to the site repeatedly. However, to ensure the success of this you have to make sure that you have a steady supply of photographs, either from yourself or from other family members

- Family news. This is another area that can attract family members regularly to the site, but again, only if it is updated regularly. Include information about events such as births, marriages and anniversaries and also achievements by family members

Don't forget

Before you start building your family website, contact as many family members as possible to see what they would like included. The more people who are involved at the outset, the more interest there will be in the final site.

How to present information

If you are in charge of producing a family website, you will have a good idea of what you want to include. The next step is to decide how to present this information. One way to do this, and one of the most effective, is to build a site with two levels of navigation. The top level will have links to all of the main subject areas within the site:

Beware

If you add links to the main navigation bar on one page, make sure that you include this updated version on all other pages too.

Once a top level link has been activated, a second level of navigation can be included, to enable navigation through this section of the site:

Writing a family history

The main part of a family website is frequently the history of the family. This is something that can start off quite small, but very quickly expand as more and more information about the family is unearthed. In many ways, writing a family history can be an addictive, and never-ending, pastime. For a family website this is very good news: if the family historian keeps unearthing new nuggets of information and adding them to the website, this can contribute to it being an evolving site rather than a static one that never changes.

Gathering what you know

A good place to start for a family history is your own knowledge. Begin by writing down everything you know about your parents, grandparents, aunts and uncles. This will provide a starting point for your family's past. Include information such as dates of birth and death, professions, military service and also geographical information. This is particularly useful if family members have lived in other countries, as you may want to access the records of these countries to find out more information.

Talking to people

Once you have written down all of the information that you know about your family, you can check and supplement this by talking to as many family members as possible. To find out information about the past, consult as many people of your own generation as possible and use their information to cross-reference details that you have written down. If you have relatives abroad you can contact them by letters or email to get them to contribute to the family history. Whenever you get new anecdotal information for the family history, double-check it if possible against another source; the passing of time can be detrimental to the exact recollection of people, places and dates.

Using objects

As well as people's own memories, physical objects can also be very useful for obtaining information about the past.

Again, go through your own objects first and pay particular attention to items, such as photographs and old books: these can reveal fascinating details about people and places plus they frequently have the names of people on the back or the inside, detailing dates that photographs were taken or books bought. As with oral history, other family members may also be able to contribute objects and if there are any birth or death certificates, military records, professional records or pension records, these can provide valuable information and clues. A lot of the time, writing a family history is a bit like a detective case: small clues can be used to reveal the bigger picture, and one thing invariably leads on to another.

Collating information

When writing a family history it is a good idea to write everything down as you remember it, or are provided with it. Otherwise you will end up with a mass of information, and collating it may become too daunting a task. Begin by breaking the information into sections. This can be by years, branches of the family or even geographical locations. Write down all of the information that you have for each section (either in longhand or on the computer), and try and keep blocks of information together. Once this has been done, it can be used to create a narrative of the family history at that point. In addition, details of individuals can be taken from this to create a graphical family tree (see pages 116–119).

Keeping it up to date

No family history is ever finished. There is always more information to find out about in the past and, obviously, there are always new, current and future events to consider. Once you have collated all of the information that you have obtained, use this as a master copy and put a date on it, so that you know when it was last updated (do this with a hard copy). Keep this for updates to your website and also for adding to when you are researching more information.

Genealogy sites

There are dozens of genealogy sites on the Web. They offer services for performing family research, and there is usually a fee for registering on the site to conduct your research. Most sites also have a lot of useful links to public records that can be used for finding family information. Some genealogy sites to look at are:

Genealogy.com at www.genealogy.com

Familysearch at www.familysearch.org

Ancestry.com at www.ancestry.com

RootsWeb.com at www.rootsweb.com

Beware

Genealogy sites are a fascinating resource, and it is easy to get side-tracked from your original quest, once you start looking through them.

Searching a site

All genealogy sites have a search facility for looking for family information. Usually, the initial search can be done without registering on the site, but after that, you will have to register to be able to access the information. To begin a genealogy search:

 Enter the details of family members in the search boxes

Click the Search button

Search

The results are displayed for the search criteria. These can be scrolled through but, usually, if you want to access further details of this information, you will have to register on the site

Researching a family history

One of the most interesting parts about writing a family history, is the research that can be undertaken. Once family members have been interviewed, you can move on to official records to expand your research. Most countries have extensive public records and some areas to consider are:

- Births, deaths and marriages

- Census records

- Military records

- Professional association records

- Court records

Thankfully, a lot of these types of records have been digitized and are now available on the Web. A search of "public records" in Google will bring up a list of numerous archives for the country in which you are living. However, for a lot of family histories, you will need to view records from a number of different countries if you find that family members have lived in different places. These can probably also be found on the Web: try amending your search by adding the country whose records you are searching for, i.e. "public records +canada".

Most genealogy sites on the Web also have extensive links to online research facilities and this can be a way to locate a lot of relevant resources. However, even if you find a lot of the required information online, it is always worth going to the physical offices of the archives which you are searching (if this is feasible). This is not only a fascinating exercise because you will see some amazing collections of records, but it may unearth some vital facts that were not included in the online site. Also, if you get the chance to speak to the people who work in the archive and records offices, they may be able to pass on some very useful ideas and tips about progressing your research further. After all, these people are professional in this line of work and probably have a wealth of experience of this type.

Creating a family tree

Once you have gathered together the information for a family tree, you can then start to create the family tree with a view to displaying it on the Web. There are two main ways to do this: with dedicated family tree software or through a genealogy site that offers a family tree creation service.

Whichever method of creating your online family tree you choose, it is a good idea to first create a hard copy version. This will give you a chance to layout all of the information in an ordered way, and you will get a much better idea of how it all fits together, before you start creating an electronic version. Also, it is very useful to have a hard copy if you are visiting public records offices, as you can use this to cross-reference any new information that you find.

Using family tree programs

There are a number of computer programs that can be used specifically to create family trees. This is usually done in a format that can be uploaded and displayed on a genealogy website. One of the most popular family tree programs is Family Tree Maker at www.familytreemaker.com:

Don't forget

A family tree program can be used to create numerous different trees. For instance, you might want to focus on one particular branch of the family. Creating several trees can be a good way to keep the whole project more manageable.

Using a genealogy site

Most genealogy sites also have a facility for creating and displaying a family tree. To do this:

1 Click the Family Trees link (this will usually be located on the site's main navigation bar)

2 General information will be displayed about creating a family tree

3 Click the Start Your Tree button

4 Enter the details of the first person in the family tree (by default this is yourself) and click the Next button

117

...cont'd

5 Enter the details for your father and click the Next button

Don't forget

With most family tree builders, you can start with any member of the family and build the tree from there.

> Ancestry.com
> Discover Your Family Story
>
> Member Login
> Username   Password (F
> Back
>
> **Start Your Family Tree**
>
> ① Step 1 ... ② **Step 2** ... ③ Step 3 ... ④ Step 4
>
> **Add Your Father**
>
> Enter what you know about your father. It's okay if you don't have all of the information. Skip this page if you don't have the information handy or you would rather fill it out later.
>
> * Required Data
>
> | | First & middle names | Last name |
> | * **Name** | Peter | Vandome |
>
> Birth date
> For example: 12 Apr 1945
>
> Birth place
> City, County, State, Country
>
> Death date
> For example: 12 Apr 1945
>
> Death place
> City, County, State, Country
>
> < Previous   Next >

6 Enter the details for your mother and click the Next button

> Ancestry.com
> Discover Your Family Story
>
> Member Login
> Username   Password (F
> Back
>
> **Start Your Family Tree**
>
> ① Step 1 ... ② Step 2 ... ③ **Step 3** ... ④ Step 4
>
> **Add Your Mother**
>
> Enter what you know about your mother. It's okay if you don't have all of the information. Skip this page if you don't have the information handy or you would rather fill it out later.
>
> * Required Data
>
> | | First & middle names | Maiden Name |
> | * **Name** | Wendy | Winifred |
>
> Birth date
> For example: 12 Apr 1945
>
> Birth place
> City, County, State, Country
>
> Death date
> For example: 12 Apr 1945
>
> Death place
> City, County, State, Country
>
> < Previous   Next >

7 Enter a name for your family tree and click the Next button. (There is usually a preview of the family tree too)

8 The first draft of the family tree is displayed. At this point it is possible to add more people, or select existing ones and edit the information about them

Inviting family members

A family website is of little use if no-one knows that it is there. Therefore, one of the first things that you should do once you have published your site, and checked that it contains everything that you want at this stage, is to let family members know about your site. One way to do this is to create an email group, using an email program such as Outlook or Outlook Express, and then send the group an invitation email containing the web address (URL) of your site. Another option, if you are using an online family website is to use the online invitation function that is available once you have created your site. To do this:

1 Enter the names and email addresses of the people you want to invite

Who would you like to participate on your site?
Each person you list below will receive an automatic e-mail invitation to participate on your site. Don't leave anyone out. If you do not have all of the required information available right now, you can add members to your site at any time in the future.

	First Name	Last Name	Gender	E-mail Address
1.	Mark	Vandome	M ▾	markvandome@hotmail.com
2.	Kirsten	Vandome	F ▾	kirstenvandome@aol.com
3.	Peter	Vandome	M ▾	petervandome@yahoo.com
4.	Wendy	Vandome	F ▾	wendyvandome@mac.com
5.	Robin	Vandome	M ▾	robinvandome@yahoo.com

2 Use the standard invitation text that is provided by the site, or write your own. Click the Continue button to send this invitation

Feel free to edit the following invitation message that will be sent on your behalf.

Come share news, photos, calendar events, family history and more with other members of this site in a private, password-protected environment. Here are just a few of the great reasons to come and join:

-- Communicate. Be in the loop with what's going on in your family, even from across the country or world.
-- Share. Easily and quickly share information, from pictures to news to a family tree.
-- Remember. Create a family calendar of birthdays and other important events, so that everyone in your family can remember them!

☑ Save changes to message for future invites

Continue

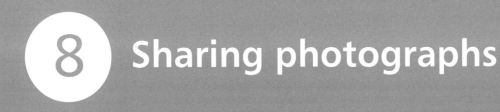

8 Sharing photographs

This chapter shows how to share family photos over the Web, including creating your own gallery.

Photos on the Web

When a photo is captured with a digital camera or a scanner it is usually in the JPEG (Joint Photographic Experts Group) format, that is indicated by the .jpg file extension. This is also a commonly used file format for use on the Web. The reason for this is that the file size of the images can be significantly compressed without losing too much image quality. However, with the power of modern digital cameras, even a lot of JPEG images are a lot bigger than they need to be for displaying on websites. Although some online services automatically resize images, large file sizes can take a long time to copy from your own computer, and it can also have a significant impact on the download time when people are viewing your website. It is, therefore, important to keep the file size of your images as small as possible. There are three main ways to do this:

- Capture the original images on a digital camera's smallest size setting (often referred to as the image resolution). Within the camera's menu this will usually be denoted by the image's physical dimensions (in pixels). So an image with pixel dimensions of 2560 x 1920 will result in a much larger file size than an image with pixel dimensions of 640 x 480. Even at this size, the image will still be displayed at a good size on a website

- Use an image editing program to save the image specifically for use on the Web. A lot of image editing programs have this facility and it greatly reduces the file size of the image. In some cases there is also an option for physically reducing the number of pixels in an image. One of the best image editing programs on the market for consumer image editing is called Photoshop Elements, from Adobe

- Use an image editing program to physically remove pixels from the image to ensure that it is displayed on a website at a reasonable size. As a general rule of thumb, the size that digital images are displayed on the Web is their physical dimensions divided by 72

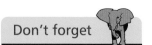

Don't forget

For general information about digital images, have a look at "Digital Photography for Seniors in Easy Steps" in this series.

Save for the Web

Using Photoshop Elements, images can quickly be saved for use on the Web. This is sometimes known as Optimization. To do this:

Don't forget

For information about Photoshop Elements, look at "Photoshop Elements 5 in Easy Steps" in this series.

1 Open a photo in Photoshop Elements

2 Select File>Save for Web command from the Menu bar

3 The Save For Web window contains options for reducing the size of the image.

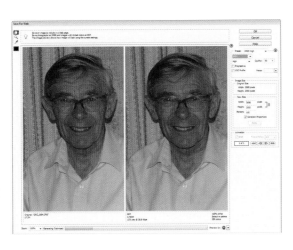

The two panels serve as a "before and after" for the edited version of the image

...cont'd

④ In the Save For Web window, select the file format (which should be JPEG) and the quality (the lower the quality, the smaller the file size)

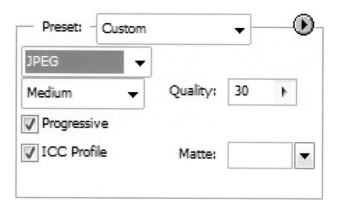

⑤ In the New Size section, enter lower pixel dimensions (Width and Height) for the image. This will ensure the image is displayed at a smaller size and also that the file size will be smaller

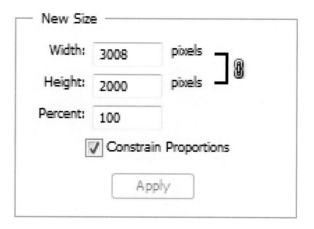

⑥ Click the OK button to save a copy of the original image

OK

Changing the pixel size

To manually change the size of an image by reducing the number of pixels (using Photoshop Elements):

1 Open an image and access the Image Size window by selecting Image>Resize>Image Size from the Menu bar

2 The Image Size window contains all of the necessary functions for changing the size of the photo

3 The dimensions (in pixels) are shown in the Pixel Dimensions section of the window

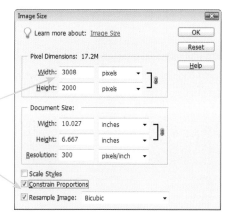

4 Check on the Resample Image and the Constrain Proportions boxes

5 Enter a lower number in the Width and Height boxes to make the photo smaller. If the Constrain Proportions box is checked, both dimensions will be changed proportionally

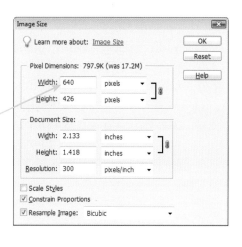

6 Click the OK button to apply the changes

Don't forget

Pixel is a contraction of "picture element" and pixels are the building blocks of digital images.

Don't forget

Resampling is the technique for changing the physical size of a digital image, by either increasing or decreasing the number of pixels.

125

Sharing on a family site

At a time when families are more geographically dispersed than ever before, the issue of online communication is one that is becoming increasingly important for families to keep in touch around the world. One of the most crucial elements of this is sharing photographs, as these are vital for family events such as births, weddings, parties, holidays and the achievements of grandchildren. There are a number of ways of sharing family photographs on websites: dedicated family websites allow you to upload your photographs so that they can be displayed on your site; if you have your own site you can design a page containing a gallery of photographs; if you just want to share photographs, there are a number of photo sharing sites that can be used for this purpose.

Using a family site

Once you have created a site on a family website, such as MyFamily.com, you can then use the facilities on the homepage to upload your photographs, i.e. copy them from your computer onto the site. To do this:

1. The Photos section of the site has options for adding photos from your computer

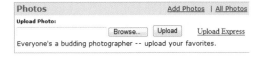

2. Click the Add Photos link

3. The Add Photos window enables you to copy photos from your own computer

4 Click the Browse button to look for photos on your computer

Browse...

5 Locate a photo on your computer

6 Click the Open button

Open

7 Repeat the process until you have selected all of the photos you want to use

Each photo has to be selected individually before it can be uploaded.

Upload Photo(s):

G:\My Documents\My Pictures Browse...
G:\My Documents\My Pictures Browse...

8 Click the Upload button to copy the photos to the website

Upload

...cont'd

9 Each photo that has been uploaded is displayed in its own window so that information can be added about them, such as a title and a description

10 Once the photo details have been added, click the Save button

11 All saved photos are displayed in a new window

12 Click a photo to view it at a larger size

13 The photos are also listed on the homepage of your site

Creating a photo gallery

If you have built your own website, it is possible to create your own photo gallery. This can be done with a site that you have created from scratch, or one created with GeoCities. When creating a photo gallery, it is a good idea to create one page that contains small versions of the photographs (thumbnails). This will allow family and friends to see if they want to look at a larger version of a particular photo. To achieve this, you will have to add a hyperlink from the thumbnail to the larger version. To create a photo gallery page, using PageBuilder in GeoCities:

Don't forget

Make sure that your thumbnail images are big enough for people to see the full subject of the image.

1 Click the New button on the Toolbar to create a new page

2 Add the text content for the photo gallery and add any page formatting, as shown in Chapter 5

...cont'd

3 Click the Pictures button on the Toolbar

4 The Select Picture window has options for copying photos from your own computer

5 Click the Upload button in the Upload Your Own Picture section

Hot tip

Create a folder on your computer into which you can save all of the photos that you will be using in your photo gallery.

6 The Upload Files window is where you can select photos to be uploaded onto your site

7 Click the Browse button

Browse...

8 Select the photos from your own computer. Once this has been done, they are displayed in the Upload Files window. Click the Upload button

9 Once your photos have been uploaded, you can select them for your current page by double-clicking on the User Files link in the Select Picture window

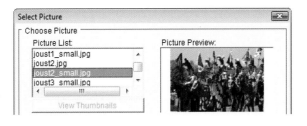

10 Select a photo in the Picture List

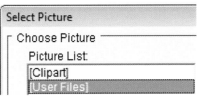

11 Click the OK button

12 The selected photo is added to your page. Repeat this for all of the photos that you want to add to the page

131

Linking to thumbnails

Once you have created a photo gallery page of thumbnails, you can then add hyperlinks to each photo, with the links going to a larger version of the photo. To do this, using PageBuilder in GeoCities:

1 Click a thumbnail image on your photo gallery page to select it

Hot tip

Enter a description near the thumbnails to instruct people what to do to access the larger versions of the thumbnails.

2 Click the Link button on the Toolbar

3 Select My File in the Hot Link window

4 Click the Choose button

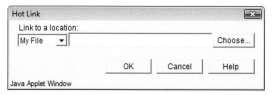

5 Select a photo in the Pick File window (this should be a file that ends with the .jpg file extension)

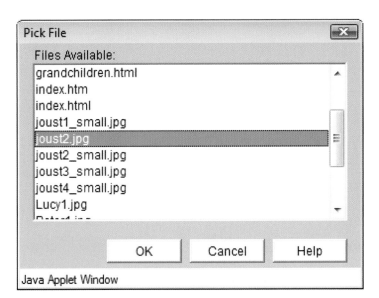

133

6 Click the OK button

7 The selected photo should be displayed in the Hot Link window

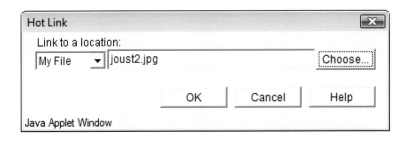

8 Click the OK button   OK

…cont'd

  Once the page is published, if you click on one of the thumbnails…

10 …the full size image will be displayed

Online sharing

If your main reason for wanting to have an online presence is to display family photographs, then another option would be to create your own photo gallery within an online photo sharing service. There are dozens of these on the Web but one of the best is called Flickr, at www.flickr.com. This is a fairly recent site, but it has already grown at an incredible rate and it has a real community feel about it. Another advantage is that it is owned by Yahoo! and if you have already signed up for GeoCities you can use the same sign in details for Flickr.

To add photos using Flickr:

1 On the Flickr homepage click the Sign up! button. If you have a GeoCities account you can sign in with these details

2 Once you have signed in, you can start adding photos to your Flickr page

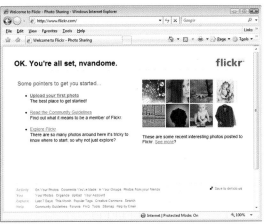

Don't forget

Flickr has a number of different services, some of which require an annual fee.

135

...cont'd

3 Click the Upload your first photo link

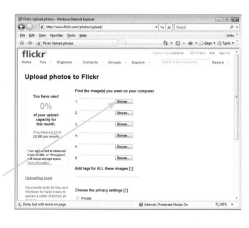

4 The Upload photos page enables you to copy photos from your computer onto the Flickr site. Click the Browse button to select a photo on your computer

5 Once the photos have been selected they are displayed in the Upload photos page

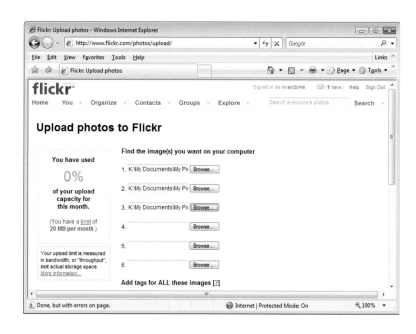

6 Scroll down the page to enter additional information about the whole group of photos that you want to add

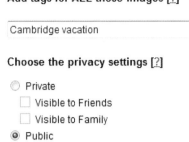

Add tags for ALL these images [?]

Cambridge vacation

Choose the privacy settings [?]

○ Private
  ☐ Visible to Friends
  ☐ Visible to Family
◉ Public

UPLOAD

7 Click the Upload button

8 Individual information can then be added for each photo, such as a title and a description

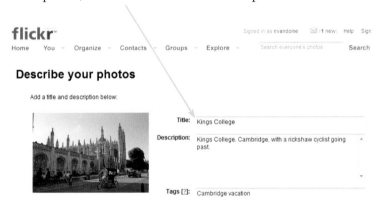

flickr

Signed in as nvandome   ✉ (1 new)   Help   Sign

Home   You ▾   Organize ▾   Contacts ▾   Groups ▾   Explore ▾   Search everyone's photos   Search

Describe your photos

Add a title and description below:

Title: Kings College

Description: Kings College, Cambridge, with a rickshaw cyclist going past.

Tags [?]: Cambridge vacation

9 All of the photos you have uploaded are displayed on your own Flickr page

137

...cont'd

Inviting people

Once you have uploaded photos to your Flickr page, you can then invite family and friends to view them. To do this:

1 Click the Contacts link on the main Flickr navigation bar

2 The Contacts page has options for inviting people

Hot tip

People can also be invited by copying the web address of your Flickr homepage and then pasting this into an email.

3 Click the Invite a friend to join link

Invite a friend to join

4 Enter the email address of the person you want to invite and also a welcome message

5 Click the Send button to send the invitation

9 Building a club site

If you are in charge of building a website for a club or a local charity, there are a lot of issues to consider. This chapter shows how best to plan, organize, build and publish a club site.

Obtaining a domain name

For anyone involved in a club, or a local charity organization, the issue of a website will invariably raise its head sooner or later. This is an excellent option for a club or charity for a number of reasons:

- The latest news can be distributed to everyone in the organization at the same time, without the need to send out a lot of hard copy letters or newsletters

- New members, or prospective members, can readily find out about the club or charity from its website

- Contact details can be displayed and updated, so people also know who to contact for various issues, i.e. the club treasurer for paying fees or the club secretary for organizing events

- There can be a facility for giving feedback, either about the club or the website or both. This does not have to be anything too complex; it can just be an email link to the person who has created the site, or anyone else in the club

When you are creating a website for a club or local charity, the first thing to decide is the domain name that you are going to use. This is the name for the whole site (individual pages within a site will contain part of the domain name but with their own specific page name) and there are two options for this:

- Create a website with an online service such as GeoCities, and add the club name onto the GeoCities domain name, i.e. www.geocities.com/ourclub/

- Buy your own unique domain name for the club, i.e. ourclub.com

Of the two, the second one is perhaps the better option since, although it costs a certain amount to register a unique domain name, it gives the website an immediately more professional appearance.

To obtain a unique domain name:

1 Find a domain name registration site by typing "domain name" into Google

2 Enter your domain name in the web address search box and click the Go button

3 If the domain name is available, you will be notified of this. Follow the onscreen instructions to register the domain name and pay for it. If the domain name is not available you will have to repeat Step 2

Agreeing the design

When you are building a website for a club, the first thing to decide on is the design of the site. This will invariably involve discussions with a number of people within the club, probably the club committee. In order to give something for everyone to discuss, it is a good idea to produce some draft proposals for people to look at, rather than just abstract concepts. These designs can be produced in sketch form, but it is preferable to have something that has been designed online, so that it is clear what the final website will look like. When you are producing a draft design, there are certain areas on which you should concentrate:

- Navigation. You should have a clear navigation structure that contains links to the main areas of the site

- Templates. Stress the need to use a standard template that will form the basis for all of the pages within the website. This will create a professional and consistent look on which the site can then be built

- Graphics. Use some graphics and photographs but emphasis that these will be used subtly and in a way to enhance the content of the site, rather than draw attention away from it

- Simplicity. Aim for a clean, clear and straightforward design that will stand the test of time. Some highly designed sites look great initially but can become tiresome after you have viewed them a few times

Have at least three different designs, using different layouts and color schemes to see what goes down the best with your audience. The final decision may come down to a vote of the club's committee, or a wider selection of club members, as it is rare for a group of people to all like the same design for a website. Don't take this personally; it could just be that someone does not like a particular color. Once the final design has been agreed, try and ensure that there is some official notification of this (ideally in the form of a club minute), to avoid any arguments at a later date.

Hot tip

Templates can be created by designing one master page and then using the Save As command in your web authoring program to save individual pages based on this master.

Draft designs

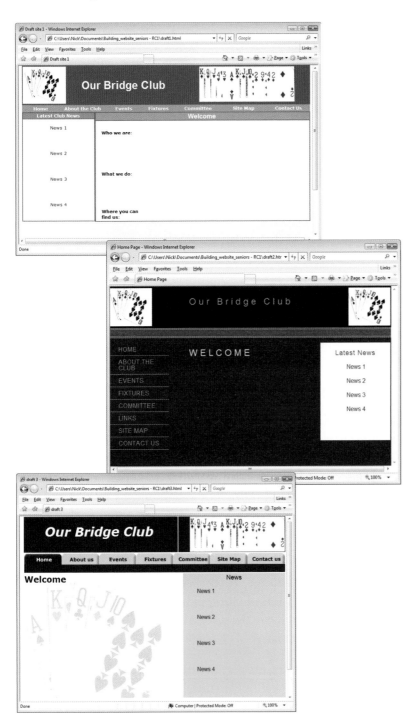

Don't forget

Create a variety of designs and don't be afraid to incorporate specific elements into another design, depending on the feedback that is given.

Agreeing the content

Once the design of the website is agreed, the next step is to decide on the content for the website. Again there are certain areas that should, generally, always be included:

- About the club information. New and prospective club members (and also a lot of existing members) will be interested to discover information about the club, such as how long it has been in existence, how to join, how the club is run and fees for belonging to the club

- Latest news. This should be posted as frequently as possible, as there is nothing worse than seeing so called latest news that is several months or years, out of date. The homepage is usually the best place for latest news as this will be the first page that most club members will access. Once one item of latest news has been superseded, or become redundant, take it off the site

- The club constitution. If your club has a constitution, then it is useful to include it on the website. But remember with this type of document, it is important to produce it in a web friendly format

- Rules and regulation. If there are rules for the activities of the club, these should be online too

- Contact details. Include as many contact details as you think are necessary. These will usually be the club post-holders, and anyone else who has an active role in the running of the club. Include email addresses but, you may want to take a collective decision about including information such as home addresses and telephone numbers, in case people are worried about their privacy

- Fixtures and outings. If your club organizes fixtures against other club or outing throughout the year, these should be listed on the site, with times, dates, places and also a contact name

All club websites are unique to their own clubs and you will know your club as well as anyone, so don't be afraid to make suggestions for what to include on the site.

Beware

Always check that people are happy to have their contact details included on the site and let them know once it has been done.

Assigning roles

Since the website is going to be for the benefit of the whole club, it is a good idea to assign different roles at the beginning of the process. If this is not done you may find that your generous offer, of designing and updating the website, has been expanded to include everything else connected with the site too. The design and upkeep of the site is a time-consuming job, so make sure there are enough volunteers to take on some of the other roles to ensure the smooth running of the site, without overwhelming you. Some areas to look at are:

- Webmaster. This is essentially your role. The webmaster is the person who builds the site and who also adds new content to the site. Over time, the webmaster is also responsible for redesigning the site so that it does not become stale

- Content manager. This is the person who is responsible for collating, or writing, the content for the site. Try not to get landed with this job yourself, as it can be a lot of work doing both. You should communicate with the content manager on a regular basis, to see if there is new club news to add to the site or, any other information that needs to be updated. Ideally, content for the site should be sent to you by email, as this will make it easier to copy and paste onto the website

- Photographer. Photographs of club activities and members are an excellent way to make a site more interesting. If someone is a keen photographer they could fulfil this role, and there are usually plenty of volunteers for this type of work. There is no reason why more than one person cannot do it

- Financial administrator. This is the person who will deal with payment for items, such as domain name registration and website hosting

Depending on the size of the club, some of these roles may be undertaken by the same person, but try and make sure that they do not all land at your feet.

Beware

Make sure that everyone knows their roles and responsibilities before you start work on the website. Otherwise you might find yourself with an increased workload, since you have the final responsibility of publishing the site.

Allocating your time

Being in charge of a club or local charity website is a responsible role, as this may be the main means of communication for a lot of people in the organization. It is therefore important, to specifically allocate your time to various areas of the evolution and maintenance of the site. Managing a good website is not something that happens by chance, it is something that has to be planned and have time spent on it.

Different areas

When considering how to spend your time on the website, there are different areas on which your time should be spent. For each, work out how much time you will need to spend, and how frequently. Keep a record of this and after a month or two, you may be able to amend it, and create an accurate timetable for all of the work that you need to do on the site to keep it working well. Some of the areas to consider include:

- Redesign. As soon as your website is up and running you should spend some of your time thinking about redesigning it. This may seem like jumping the gun slightly, but it is good practise to redesign, or revamp, a website every 1–2 years, and you will be surprised how quickly this comes around. Look at other websites for new design features that you like, and which you think you can produce yourself, and make a note of these for future reference

- Weekly maintenance. This includes items such as club news and current activities. For this, keep a "Last Updated" date on the relevant pages, and update the date whenever you check the page, even if there is no new information. This will show people that the page is being actively maintained

- Monthly maintenance. This can be general housekeeping, such as making sure that all information is still relevant, and that items like contact details are still up to date

Hot tip

Keep a list of favorite websites that you can use as reference when it comes to updating your site. These can be stored as Favorites within a web browser, such as Internet Explorer or Firefox.

Creating updating guidelines

In many ways, the easy part is building a website; the hard part is keeping it interesting and current. Once you have decided how you are going to spend your time working on the website, it is a good idea to create guidelines for how the site should be updated. This will be useful for yourself to refer to from time to time, but it will be invaluable for the next person who is responsible for maintaining the website: the experience of a previous webmaster can be a lot more worthwhile than a lot of technical jargon. Some items to include in updating guidelines:

- Identify items that should be updated on a weekly, monthly or annual basis. Use reminders, either electronic or hard copy, to make sure that none of these dates are missed (this can be particularly easy to do with annual events, such as updating the names of the club's committee members and postholders)

- When new pages are created, identify who is responsible for the content of the pages

- Give relevant pages a "last updated" date and also a "next review due" date. Make sure the pages are looked at on these dates and updated accordingly, even if there is no new information to include

- Email people who are responsible for certain areas of information on the site. Set up a timetable for how regularly you contact them, and let them know you will be contacting them in this way

- Look for redundant/out of date data. If old information is found, remove it from the site, but make sure you inform the relevant people that this has been done

- Create a timetable for a full review of the site. A good time period for this is about a year, because this will give you time to canvas opinion about the site, and then redesign it if necessary. It can easily take six months from reviewing a website to a new version appearing

Don't forget

Keep an electronic version of your updating guidelines, so that you can email them to anyone who is interested.

Adding content

If you are building a club or local charity website, there is a good chance that the organization will have its own domain name and also hosting service. If this is the case, you may not be able to add the content for the site using an online service, such as GeoCities. The other available options are using an HTML editor, such as Composer, or a professional program such as Dreamweaver. With both of these a certain knowledge of HTML is required.

Using Composer

Composer is an HTML editor and is part of the Mozilla Suite of programs that also includes a web browser and an email program. It can be freely downloaded at www.mozilla. org/products/mozilla1.x/

Once it is downloaded, Composer can be accessed from the Mozilla browser by selecting Window>Composer from the Menu bar.

Composer is an HTML editor, which means you can add content and the program helps with the creation of the HTML and, in a lot of cases, inserts the relevant HTML tags. You can view the page in normal mode, with the HTML tags showing (see below), just the HTML or in Preview mode. This is a good option for a first experience with HTML.

Don't forget

Composer is a good way to learn about the basics of HTML, while still being able to create content in a graphical interface.

Using Dreamweaver

Dreamweaver is a professional web authoring program from Adobe (formerly produced by Macromedia), which is the most powerful program of its kind on the market. However, there is a steep learning curve to Dreamweaver and it is not for the faint-hearted. But once you have mastered building web pages in other programs, it may present a sufficient challenge as the next step of your web development.

Dreamweaver comes with numerous pre-designed templates on which pages can be based. It also contains a lot of panels and inspectors for adding content to pages. Once these are fully mastered, almost anything can be added to a web page.

The content in Dreamweaver can be viewed in Design View, which allows you to add content as it will appear on the Web, or in Code View, which is the source code for the content, or in both (see below).

Don't forget

For more information about Dreamweaver, have a look at "Dreamweaver 8 in Easy Steps".

149

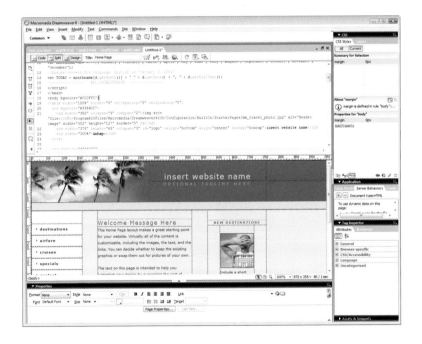

Finding a web host

Most hosting services will host an existing domain name and they will also offer a service for registering a domain name and hosting your site. Usually, obtaining your domain name registration and hosting from the same site is cheaper than doing it with two separate suppliers.

There are hundreds of companies that offer web hosting services, and they frequently have different price schemes and services, depending on the type of website that you want hosted. For a fairly straightforward club site, the standard, i.e. least expensive scheme will almost certainly be sufficient. For more complex sites (usually business sites), then more expensive and high-powered schemes may be required.

When you are looking for a web host, type "website hosting" into Google and look through at least half a dozen sites, to see the different prices and services on offer. Most web hosting services have a homepage that details the company's services, and a Sign Up button, that can be used to register your site for hosting (see below).

Don't forget

Even though it involves spending money, the task of finding a web hosting service will invariably fall to the club's webmaster. Just make sure that you are reimbursed for any money that you spend.

Search engine registration

Once your club or local charity site has been designed, built and uploaded to a hosting service, the next thing to think about is to register your site with a search engine. This will add your site's web address to the search engine's index, so that it should show up when people search using keywords that include the subject of your site. Sites can be registered with most major search engines, and there is usually a link on the search engine's site that can be followed to register a website. To do this (for Google):

1 On the homepage click the About Google link

About Google

2 Click the Submit your content to Google link in the For Site Owners box

For Site Owners

Advertising
AdWords, AdSense...

Business Solutions
Google Search Appliance, Google Mini, WebSearch...

Webmaster Central
One-stop shop for comprehensive info about how Google crawls and indexes websites...

Submit your content to Google
Add your site, Google Base, Google Sitemaps...

Don't forget

Do not become too fixated with search engine registration and search listings (the position your site appears when certain keywords are searched for). An equally effective way of getting people to view your site is through word of mouth.

3 Click the Add your URL to Google's Index link

Add your URL to Google's index
We add and update new websites to our index every time we crawl the web; we invite you to submit your top-level URL to make sure we don't miss your site.

4 Enter the full URL and any comments about your site

URL: http://www.nybridgeclub.com

Comments: For anyone interested in contract bridge in th

5 Click the Add URL button

Add URL

...cont'd

Multiple registrations

Another option for search engine registration, is to use a service that submits your site's URL to multiple sites at the same time. One of the most widely used is SubmitExpress at www.submitexpress.com. To submit to multiple sites:

 On the homepage, enter your site's URL and click the Continue button

Free Webmaster Tools

FREE SUBMISSION
Free Submission to 40+ Search Engines

| www.nybridgeclub.com | Continue |

 Enter the full URL of the site and a contact email address for the site

 FREE Website Submission

Our submission script will submit your website URL to 20+ top search engines for free, including Google. Click here for search engines list and details

Before you submit to the search engines, CLICK HERE to make sure you are using the right keywords within your meta tags. Then make sure that you take advantage of our free META Tag Generator for best placement. Please do not submit your URL more than once a month. Multiple submissions of the same URL to some search engines could be considered spamming and therefore may ban you from being listed.

| * **URL:** | http://www.nybridgeclub.com |
| * **Email:** | nybridgeclub@hotmail.com |

 Click the Submit button

Submit

10 Creating a family blog

One of the great things about the Web is that it is continually evolving. A recent development is that of blogs, or web logs. This chapter explains what blogs are all about and shows how to create, edit and manage them using freely available tools on the Web.

What is a blog

The word "blog" is one of the less elegant terms to have been invented on the World Wide Web but, it is a phenomenon that has spread rapidly in the last few years. Blogs have been in existence on the Web since about 2000 and the term is a contraction of "web log", which is essentially an online diary. These are created by individuals, usually on dedicated blog sites, and they can cover anything from your favorite pet to your latest holiday.

Blogs are generally updated regularly, with a lot of them being updated on a daily basis. This gives them an immediacy that attracts large numbers of readers. Some of this is because of a genuine sense of interest, but some of it is also probably a bit voyeristic: most of us have a secret urge to read other people's diaries and blogs are a legitimate online way in which to do this.

In their early days, blogs generally just contained text, but now the software used to create blogs can include photographs and, in some cases, video.

Despite the way that blogs have taken off on the Web, there is still a sense of community about them, as if people see this as a free-sprited side of the Web, where people can freely share thoughts, ideas and opinions. On some sites, blogs covering similar topics are grouped together so that like-minded people can share their views with each other. Most blogs also have a facility whereby people can give you feedback on your blog and also contribute their own thoughts and views to your page.

Blogs are fairly new in terms of the World Wide Web, but they have already had a significant impact on the political and social landscape around the world. Rarely does a day now go by without some kind of news story relating to information that is contained within a blog. As far as blogs in the family environment are concerned, they are a great way to share information, keep in touch and generate topical debate about family issues.

Don't forget

Even if you never create a blog, they are a good thing to know about, as they are becoming more widely used and talked about.

What to write about

Once you start a blog, it is yours and it is up to you, as to what you want to write about. However, there are some general areas that you should think about avoiding:

- Anything that may upset or embarrass any other family members or friends. Remember, blogs can be read by anyone, so a small indiscretion could have major consequences

- Never reveal significant personal information on a blog, such as any financial information

- Be careful not to offend anyone on the grounds of race, religion or sexuality

So what are good topics for a family blog?

- Start with the family. Blogs are a great way to not only pass on general family information and your views of your latest grandchild, they are also excellent forums for discussing the organization of family occasions, such as weddings or anniversaries. Suggestions can be posted on a blog for other family members to view and comment on, and any contentious points can be discussed on the blog. This is an excellent way in which to keep everyone involved in the organization of events and, it ensures that no-one feels left out or that they have not had a chance to voice their opinion

- Vacation blogs. Blogs can be used to update family and friends about your vacations, while you are still on them without the need to wait until you get home. They are particularly useful for longer vacations, such as cruises. Since most blogs are created by online sites, you can update them wherever there is an Internet connection. All you have to do is logon to your blogging site and then dazzle people with your latest vacation news

- Hobby blogs. A blog of your favorite hobby is a great way to keep like-minded people aware of what you are up to and you will probably get some useful feedback too from other hobbyists

Don't forget

You do not necessarily have to write a blog aimed at anyone; it can just be your own personal online diary.

Designing with Blogger

When it comes to designing a blog, a lot of the hard work is already done for you. There are a number of online websites that will design and host a blog for you, usually for free. The largest blogging site on the Web is called Blogger and this can be accessed at www.blogger.com

Creating an account

Before you can start working on your blog, you have to first create an account, which is free. To do this:

1 On the Blogger homepage click the Create Your Blog Now button

Create a **blog** in 3 easy steps:

1 Create an account

2 Name your blog

3 Choose a template

CREATE YOUR BLOG NOW

2 Enter your details including a user name, a password, a display name (the name that will be displayed on the blog when viewed on the Web) and an email address

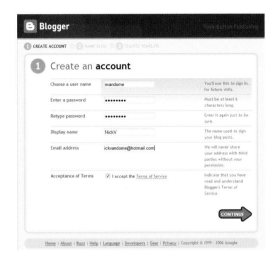

3 Click the Continue button

4 Enter a name and web address (URL) for your blog and enter the Word Verification code (this ensures that it is not an automated entry and that it is an individual)

5 Click the Continue button

Don't forget

You can create several different blogs within Blogger, but each one has to have its own unique name and web address (URL).

157

...cont'd

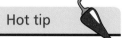

Hot tip

A blog's template can be changed at any time. To do this, login to your blog and select Templates>Pick New.

Don't forget

Blogger templates are actually stylesheets used to format the content on the page. For more on stylesheets, see Chapter 11.

6 Select a template design for your blog. This will appear as the blog's design once it is published and viewed on the Web. It does not appear during posting

7 Click the Continue button

8 You will receive a message to tell you that the blog has been created

9 Click the Start Posting button to begin adding content to your blog

Posting to a blog

Once you have registered on Blogger.com and clicked on the Start Posting button, as shown on the previous page, you can then start posting to your blog. To do this:

1 Enter a title for the post and then enter the text that you want displayed

2 Click here to select text font and size

3 Click here to add bold and italic formatting to the text

4 Click here to select colors for the text

5 Click the Preview link to see how the text formatting will appear

Preview

Beware

When a post is previewed it only shows the text formatting. The page is not displayed within its selected template.

...cont'd

6 Click the Publish Post button

Publish Post

7 A window will alert you to the fact that the blog has been published

When a blog is published on Blogger, it has the name "blogspot" as part of its web address, e.g. myblog.blogspot.com

8 Click the View Blog link

View Blog

9 The published blog is displayed on the Web

Don't forget

Once a blog has been published, check it to make sure that you are happy with its appearance.

Editing a blog

After you have made your first post to your blog you can logout, leaving the post on the Web for anyone else to see. However, due to the nature of blogs you will probably want to return to it at regular intervals to add new posts or edit the ones that you have already created. To do this:

1 Click the Sign in to Blogger link on the homepage

2 Enter your login details and click on the Sign In button

3 The Dashboard window is displayed. This shows details about your blogs and offers options for editing and amending them

Don't forget

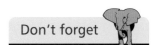

If you create more than one blog, they will all be displayed within the Dashboard.

161

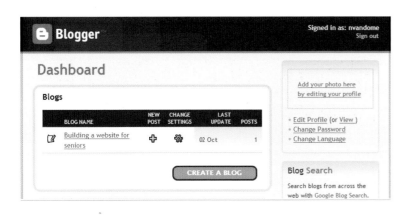

...cont'd

4   Click the link for an existing blog

5   Details of the selected blog are displayed

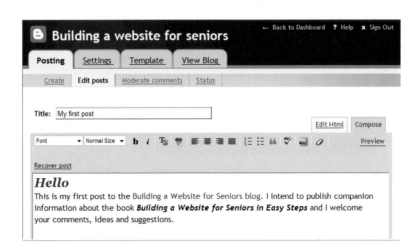

6   Click the Edit button to edit a post on the blog

7   The selected post is displayed

8 Make editing changes to the post

9 Click the Publish Post button to publish the new version of the post

Publish Post

10 The edited post is displayed on the blog

Beware

Try not to edit the same post too many times. This is because if people have read an earlier version they may feel that they have seen inaccurate information.

Creating a new blog

You do not have to restrict yourself to a single blog. It is possible to create different blogs, covering different subjects, such as family, travel and hobbies. To create a new blog:

 1 Login to Blogger and within the Dashboard window, click the Create a Blog button

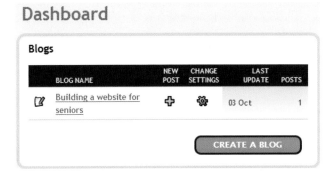

164

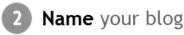 **2** Enter a title and an address for the new blog

3 Complete the Word Verification box

4 Click the Continue button

5 Select a template for your new blog by checking on the button next to the name

preview template

Don't forget

Use different templates for each new blog. This will create a separate identity for each blog.

6 Click the Continue button

CONTINUE

7 A new window announces that the new blog has been created

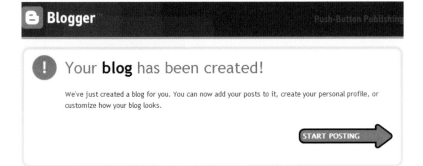

B Blogger™   Push-Button Publishing

! Your **blog** has been created!

We've just created a blog for you. You can now add your posts to it, create your personal profile, or customize how your blog looks.

START POSTING

8 Click the Start Posting button to create a post for your new blog

START POSTING

Adding a new post

Blogs are designed to be updated regularly, so once your blog is up and running, you will want to add new posts to keep the content fresh and make it interesting for people who are continually looking at your blog. To add a new post:

1 In the Dashboard section click the New Post button; or

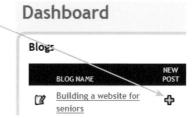

2 Access an existing blog and click the Create new post button

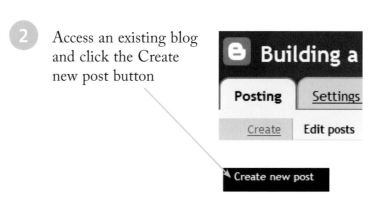

3 Enter the content for the new post

4 Click the Publish Post button to add the post to your blog

Adding images

Blogs have evolved considerably since their early days and now, as well as text, images can also be added to blogs to give them an extra graphical dimension. To do this:

1 Create a post containing the relevant text

2 Click here on the Toolbar to select an image

3 The Upload Images window displays options for adding images to your blog

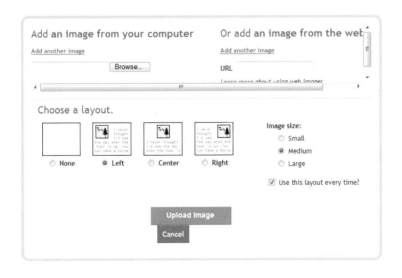

...cont'd

4 Click the
Browse button
to select an image
from your own
computer

Add **an image from your computer**

Add another image

_____ Browse...

5 Once the image
is selected it is
displayed here

Add **an image from your computer**

Add another image

G:\My Documents\My Pic Browse...

6 Select a layout
design for the image

Choose a layout.

○ None   ○ Left   ○ Center   ◉ Right

Hot tip

Try selecting different
layouts when
publishing a post,
to see how the
photos appear in the
published version.

7 Click the
Upload Image
button

8 While the image is being uploaded the following
window is displayed

Loading

Your images are being uploaded to Blogger.

9 Once the image has been added, click the Done button

10 The image is added to the post before it has been published

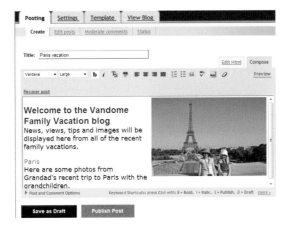

Don't forget

Regardless of its original size, a photo will be resized to appear at a standard size in a post.

169

11 Click the Publish Post button

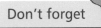

12 The image is displayed within the published post on the blog. The formatting may look slightly different from the editing environment

Adding links

Since blogs are published on the World Wide Web, they can be linked to other pages on the Web in the same way as pages on any other website. This is done by adding hyperlinks to elements within a post on the blog. To do this:

1 Create a new post or open an existing one for editing. Highlight a piece of text

Welcome to
News, views, tij
family vacation:

Paris
Here are some
grandchildren.

2 Click here on the Toolbar to add a link

3 The Hyperlink window displays options for the type of link to be added. If it is another web page, the type of link will usually be http:

4 Open the web page to which you want to link. Highlight the address in the Address Bar and select Edit>Copy from the Menu bar

5　Double-click in the URL box in the

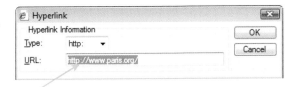

Hyperlink window and select Edit>Paste from the Menu bar

6　Click the OK button

7　The selected piece of text is converted into a hyperlink, which is denoted by underlining

Paris
Here are
grandchil

8　When the post is published, the link becomes active

nere from all or

Paris
Here are some p
trip to Paris with

9　Once the link is activated, i.e. clicked on, the linked page will open

Beware

When you double-click in the URL box, make sure the "http://" is highlighted. Otherwise you will have "http://" twice in the URL box and this will be an invalid web address.

Adding family members

If you are creating a family blog, it makes sense to give your family members special access. This can be done by creating them as members and then they can have special privileges set for them, such as being allowed to post on your blog. To add family members:

1. Open a blog and click the Settings tab and then the Members button

2. This section has options for adding people

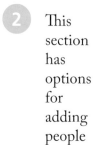

3. Click the Add Team Member(s)

4. Enter the email addresses of the people who you want to add

5. Enter a message that will be sent to the people who have been added

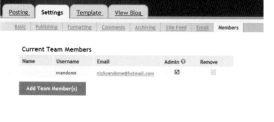

6. Click the Save Settings button to complete adding new members to your blog

Working with comments

Allowing people to comment on blogs is one of the ways in which they can become truly interactive. However, you have a certain amount of control over how comments are added and displayed on your blog.

1 Once a blog is published,

posted by NickV @ 2:28 AM 0 comments

comments can be added by clicking on the Comments link at the bottom of each post

2 Comments can be added to the Leave your comment box

Beware

If you receive an inflammatory comment, do not reply to it immediately as you may be too annoyed to give a rational response. Better to calm down and reply in a more measured manner at a later date.

Managing comments

To determine how comments are added to your blogs and how they are displayed:

1 Open a blog and click the Settings tab and the Comments button

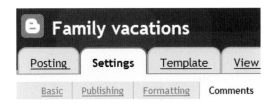

...cont'd

(2) Check on the Show button to enable comments on your blog to be displayed

Comments   ● Show   ○ Hide

(3) Click in the Who Can Comment? box to select users who can leave comments

Who Can
Comment?   Only Registered Users   ▼

(4) Select who you want to be able to comment on your blog. This is where you can specify that only members of the blog can leave comments

Only Registered Users
Anyone
Only Members of this Blog

(5) Click the Save Settings button to keep the changes that have been made

Save Settings

Blogging on GeoCities

If you have created a website using GeoCities, you will be able to use your login to create a GeoCities blog. To do this:

1 Once you have logged in to GeoCities, click the Start a Blog link within the Control Panel

Start a Blog
Set up and start publishing a basic web log.

2 Click the Standard button to create the default type of blog

Standard

Enter a title and description, then decide whether to make your blog your home page, and we'll set up your blog using a standard design. (Recommended for most users.)

Standard

3 Enter a name, title and description for your blog. Click the Next button

Activate a Blog: Standard

1. Choose blog settings.
Select a nickname to represent yourself on Yahoo! 360°, then enter a title and short description to appear on every page of your blog.

Nickname: Nick V
Title: Nick V's Blog
Description: My thoughts about family and friends.

83 characters left. Limit 120 characters.

2. Choose whether to make your blog your home page.
Check the box below to replace your current home page with your blog. Visitors will access your blog at http://geocities.com/nvandome.

☐ Make my blog my home page.

[Next >] [Cancel]

4 Click the Activate button

Activate a Blog: Standard

3. Confirm Terms of Service.
You're almost done! Review and acknowledge the Terms of Service by checking the box below. When you're ready, click the "Activate" button to complete setup of your blog.

☑ By checking this box, I acknowledge that I have read, understand, and agree to the Yahoo! Small Business Consolidated Terms of Service.

[< Back] [**Activate**] [Cancel]

Hot tip

A GeoCities blog can be set as your homepage for your GeoCities website, i.e. the blog becomes your site's index page. To do this, check on the Make my blog my home page box, underneath the section for the blog's name and description.

...cont'd

5 Click the Compose a blog entry (post) link

Activate a Blog: Next Steps

Congratulations, you successfully activated your blog!

To view or begin working on your blog, choose one of the following links:

Compose a blog entry (post)
Edit blog settings
View your blog

6 Add content for the post. This can include formatted text and images

Post a New Blog Entry
Your entry can consist of text, a photo, or both. Each entry must have a title.

New Entry

Entry title:
Entry for October 3, 2006

Photo:
Browse...
Be sure your photo is a JPEG file no larger than 3MB. Click "Preview" to see this photo.

Entry content:

This is my first blog entry.

View HTML Source. Most HTML is OK. Learn more.

Preview | Post This Entry | Cancel

7 Click the Post This Entry button

Post This Entry

8 Click the View your blog link

View your blog

9 The blog is displayed on the Web

Nick V's Blog

My thoughts about family and friends.

View: Text & Photos | Photos only | Text only
Entries: 1 - 1 of 1 First | < Prev | Next > | Last

Entry for October 3

This is my first blog entry.

2006-10-03 11:44:51 GMT   Comments: 0 | Permanent Link

View: Text & Photos | Photos only | Text only
Entries: 1 - 1 of 1 First | < Prev | Next > | Last

Site Home

Beware

The designs for GeoCities blogs are more limited than those for a dedicated blogging site, such as Blogger.

11 Taking the next steps

This chapter shows how to develop your web design skills and knowledge.

HTML overview

HyperText Markup Language (HTML) is the computer code used to create web pages. It is not a fully-blown computer programming language, but rather a set of instructions that enables a web browser to determine the layout of pages.

HTML is created by using a series of tags, which contain the instructions that are interpreted by web browsers. These tags are placed around the item to which you want that particular command to apply. Most tags, but not all of them, have an opening and a closing element. The opening tag contains the particular command and the closing tag contains the same command, but with a / in front of it, to denote the end of the command. For instance, if you wanted to display a piece of text as bold, you could do it with the following piece of HTML:

This text would appear bold in a browser

HTML is a text-based code which means that the source HTML file only contains text and not images or multimedia items. These appear in the browser because of a reference to them that is placed in an HTML document. For instance, if you wanted to include an image in a document, you would insert the following piece of HTML into your source file:

<img src="myimage.jpg">

This would instruct the browser to insert this image at the required point within the HTML document when it is being viewed on the Web. It is possible to insert HTML code to instruct a variety of graphics and multimedia files to be displayed in a web page. However, it is important to remember that when you are publishing your pages, all of the items that are referred to in the source HTML document are uploaded to the website hosting service as well as the HTML file, i.e. all image files have to be uploaded in order for them to be displayed in a web browser.

Don't forget

A page's HTML code can be inspected by viewing the page in a browser and selecting View>Source (Internet Explorer) from the Menu bar.

Common tags

Unless otherwise stated, tags use the equivalent closing tag by inserting / in front of the command. Some of the most commonly used tags in HTML are:

- <p> This creates a new paragraph

- <strong> This creates bold text

- <em> This creates italics

- <u> This creates underlined text

-
  This inserts a line break (this does not have a closing tag)

- <hr> This inserts a horizontal line (this does not have a closing tag)

- <img src="image.jpg"> This inserts the specified image

- <font face="Arial"> This specifies a particular font. The closing tag is just </font>

- <h1> This formats text at a preset heading size. There are six levels for this: h1 being the largest and h6 being the smallest. Paragraph and other formatting tags cannot be used within heading tags

- <table> This inserts a table

- <color="ffffff"> This can be used to select a color for a variety of items, including background color and text color

- <a href="default.htm">Home Page</a> This is used to create a hyperlink to another web page. In this case the link is to the file "default.htm" and the words "Home Page" will appear underlined on the web page, denoting that it is a link to another page

Don't forget

HTML is relatively forgiving and, unlike some fully-blown computer languages, if a tag is omitted or placed in the wrong place, it will not result in the whole file becoming unusable.

Anatomy of an HTML file

To see how HTML files work, the code can be dissected to identify the different elements in the file.

HTML content

Every HTML file is contained within the HTML tags: <html></html>. This tells the browser, that is displaying the file, that it is viewing an HTML file and should display it accordingly.

Head content

The Head content in HTML files is generally information that does not appear in the published document. This covers items such as meta data (which is used by search engines to identify the content on the site), the file's title, any stylesheets to which the file is linked (see pages 182–184 for more details) and any computer scripts that have been associated with the page. The Head content appears at the beginning of the code between the <head></head> tags:

```
<head>

<title>Vandome Family Website</title>

<meta name="Keywords" content="Vandome, history, France, Canada, Australia." />

<meta name="description" content="This is the website for the Vandome family.
It contains family news, history, a family tree and a global photo gallery." />

<link href="2col_rightNav.css" rel="stylesheet" type="text/css" />
</head>
```

The title is the only part of the Head content that is visible when the page is published, and this appears at the top left of the browser window in which the page is displayed:

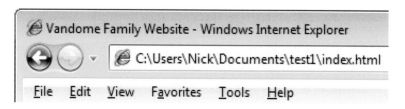

Don't forget

As far as search engines are concerned, the most important element of the HEAD content are the Keywords and the Description. These are used to correspond to search terms entered by users.

Body content

After the Head content, all of the rest of the content within an HTML file is contained within the Body content, which is represented by the <body></body> tags. All of the content that is displayed is contained within the body tag. In the following example the <h1> tag is used to specify the size of the largest heading, the <p> tag is used to denote a new paragraph, the <strong> tag is used to create bold text and the <h3> and <h4> tags are used to specify smaller headings:

```
<body>
<h1>This is Heading 1</h1>
<p>This is body text</p>
<p><strong>This is bold body text</strong></p>
<h3>This is Heading 3</h3>
<h4>This is Heading 4</h4>
</body>
```

When viewed in a browser, this Body content would look like this:

With no content on a page, the html, head and body tags would look like this:

```
<html>

<head>
</head>

<body>
</body>

</html>
```

Using stylesheets

In the early days of web design the majority of pages were created with only HTML code. This specified the content and formatting within the same document. However, this could be cumbersome, in that each time there was a change in formatting, this would have to be included in the HTML document. For instance, each time a different font is used, it had to be specified in terms of the font family, size and color. If there are a lot of different font styles, sizes and colors this can lead to a lot of code in the HTML file.

In recent years stylesheets (Cascading Style Sheets or CSS) have become a lot more popular for designing web pages. This is because they can be used to separate the content and presentation of web pages. The content is still in the HTML document but the presentation (or formatting) is included within the stylesheet document, in the form of a group of formatting rules. These can then be applied to multiple files. This means that if one of the rules is updated, the relevant content in all of the linked files is also updated, without the need to edit the individual HTML files. Stylesheets can be used for formatting and positioning of all items within an HTML file, including text, backgrounds, tables and images.

Stylesheets can be imported directly into an HTML file, in which case they are usually located in the <head> section of the document, or they can be created in specific stylesheet files. These have a .css extension and can be linked to the HTML file. This means that the HTML file takes all of its formatting from the stylesheet. For instance, if an HTML file has been created with unformatted body text and specific heading styles, these tags will be recognized by a linked stylesheet and the relevant tags will then take the formatting from the stylesheet.

Creating stylesheets can be a complex business and, if possible, it is better to use stylesheets that have already been created. Some web authoring programs contain sample stylesheets.

Don't forget

For more information about stylesheets, have a look at "CSS in Easy Steps" in this series.

How stylesheets work
Stylesheets work by applying formatting to HTML files:

1   Enter plain content into an HTML file

This is Heading 1

This is body text

This is bold body text

This is Heading 3

This is Heading 4

2   A stylesheet can be linked to an HTML file by entering the relevant code in the HEAD of the HTML file

```
<head>

<title>Vandome Family Website</title>

<meta name="Keywords" content="Vandome, history, France, Canada, Australia." />

<meta name="description" content="This is the website for the Vandome family.
It contains family news, history, a family tree and a global photo gallery." />

<link href="CSS/Level3_3.css" rel="stylesheet" type="text/css" />

</head>
```

Don't forget

Stylesheets can also be embedded in an individual file, but this means that if the stylesheet is edited the changes will only apply to the file in which the stylesheet is located.

3   Once the stylesheet has been attached, its formatting is applied to the content in the HTML file

This is Heading 1

This is body text

This is bold body text

This is Heading 3

This is Heading 4

Updating stylesheets

One of the great advantages of using stylesheets is that, if they are attached to numerous HTML files, individual elements can be updated once in the stylesheet and this will be applied to all of the linked HTML files, without having to update each file individually. To do this:

1 Open a stylesheet file and locate an element which you want to change (in this example it will be color for all body text)

```
body {
    background-color: #FFFFCC;
    font-family: Verdana, Arial, Helvetica, sans-serif;
    font-size: 12px;
    line-height: 24px;
    color: #336699;
}
```

Beware

Stylesheet files are a lot less forgiving than HTML ones in terms of accuracy: if you make a single syntax error in a stylesheet file, the whole stylesheet will cease to function.

2 Make editing changes to the selected element

```
color: #FF0099;
```

3 The changes in the stylesheet are applied to this element in all of the HTML files to which the stylesheet is attached

This is Heading 1

This is body text

This is bold body text

This is Heading 3

This is Heading 4

Publishing with FTP

If you are building and publishing a website that has its own domain name (web address) and is being hosted by an online hosting service, you will need a way in which to copy the website files from your own computer onto the computers of the hosting service. The most common way of doing this is through a method called FTP (File Transfer Protocol). This is a protocol (an agreed format for transferring data) for exchanging files on the Internet. All types of files can be transferred using FTP, so for web publishing it is possible to transfer all of the relevant files, such as HTML files and image files.

There are a number of dedicated FTP programs that can be downloaded for free from the Web. The process for using these programs is to define a website on your own computer (usually by specifying a folder on your computer that contains all of your website files), and then transfering all of the files to the remote computer, i.e. the one of the hosting service. In order to do this you will need various settings, such as the address of the hosting service's computer and a password, but these will be given to you when you register with a hosting service. To find FTP programs on the Web, enter "FTP programs" into Google:

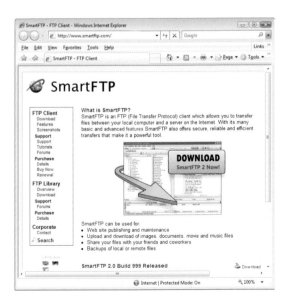

...cont'd

FTP with a web authoring program

Instead of using a dedicated FTP program, some web authoring programs also have a built-in FTP function. These are usually the more advanced programs, such as Dreamweaver. To publish a website in this way:

1   Open the Site files window in the program. The files that are stored on your computer are shown here

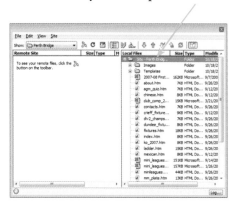

2   Select the site's main folder, and click on the Put button to publish your website to the remote hosting service

3   The site files are displayed here and these can now be viewed on the Web

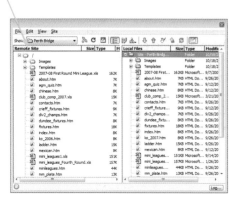

Index